STRANGE HAPPENINGS

A PARANORMAL INVESTIGATOR'S STORY

DAN HAMMOND

BEYOND THE FRAY
Publishing

ISBN 13: 978-1-954528-23-9

Cover design: Disgruntled Dystopian Publications

Beyond The Fray Publishing, a division of Beyond The Fray, LLC, San
Diego, CA
www.beyondthefraypublishing.com

BEYOND THE FRAY

Publishing

CONTENTS

DEDICATED TO ALL THE HAMMOND SPIRITS OUT THERE...

ACKNOWLEDGMENTS

Your life can take a very funny turn at times. One minute you are sitting there dead set on a certain type of future, and then the next minute you have been derailed and launched into something totally foreign and new. This is what happened to me...

Just over two years ago, I was at a friend's house, having a couple of beers. He left to go attend to something and flipped me the TV remote and said to help myself. I fumbled through the channels and found myself on a show that involved four paranormal investigators creeping around in the dark and using crazy-looking gadgets that I had never seen before. These four men jumped at every little noise, saw shadows moving about, and caught ghostly voices on their recorders. I instantly knew that I wanted to do what they were doing. I just didn't know where to begin.

Weeks later, I expressed an interest in the paranormal to my neighbor Jenn during a conversation in regard to a very haunted-looking home in our neighborhood. She, in turn, told me that a friend of hers was a ghost hunter and she would connect the two of us. Before long, I was a part of the paranormal group SHIP (Strange Happenings Investigators of the Paranormal). It all happened so quickly and so easily.

From there, I became good friends with many great people who shared my interests. We all got along very well, and there was nowhere to go but forward. Forward for me was to become one of three hosts of a paranormal podcast, being featured on two well-known supernatural television shows, and presenting paranormal evidence in front of sold-out venues.

I want to thank ALL the members of SHIP for their friendship and exciting times. John K for helping me tap into my psychic gifts (or was it psycho?), Danny B for being our wonderful tech guy on the podcast (and fellow host), and to all the people who allowed me into their homes and establishments to bang around in the dark and talk to the air.

To my wife, Ana, for putting up with my crazy hobbies and adventures, and to my two kids, whom I had to continually lie to as to where I was going that evening.

And to all the cool ghosts and spirits out there who have helped me along the way, guided me, and put suggestions in all our ears – ever so slightly.

There are no coincidences in life...

INTRODUCTION

People love to be scared. They are drawn to the excitement of fear, and the adrenaline that it can produce. Whether you get your chills and thrills from bungee jumping, roller coasters, or horror movies, it's a raw emotion that many actively seek. Although personally, I am not much of a thrill seeker, I have never shied away from anything that others might perceive as frightening. Yet, when it comes to the paranormal, things are a little different for me.

For me it's more of a way to show that I'm not scared, although I have been reminded many times that I should be. As someone with a former law enforcement background, I would ignore the base rational thoughts, ignore the flight response, and try to always be the first one through the door. I have been stabbed, shot at, jumped by gang members, and taken all sorts of abuse, both physical and mental. When it came to my "career" in ghost hunting – nothing changed. I wanted to be in the thick of things. I wanted to be left alone in the dark damp cellar or attic by myself. I wanted something to crawl up my back and make itself known. I would silently wish that some unseen force would leave claw marks down my arm. I wanted to show the spirit world that I could take whatever it threw at me. So far, I have.

The stories that I am going to tell you in this book are absolutely true. I know that could be an easy lie, but it's not. If anyone has access to a polygraph machine, then I would be more than happy to have you hook me up and ask away. I'm sure that we would both be amazed at the results. I will admit that there are moments when even I have a tough time believing them myself. I only ask that you keep an open mind and think about all the other crazy paranormal stories you have heard over the years. Almost everyone has a story to tell.

Even though I personally believe that many paranormal topics are real, they are almost impossible to prove. Professional skeptics and naysayers alike will do their best to refute any type of nonscientific "evidence" and quickly dismiss it. Like organized religion though, you gotta have faith. There are many things in this world that we will never fully understand and may never be able to prove. Even with the amount of "evidence" out there, we will still have the hardcore skeptics who will try their best to debunk everything that may present itself as paranormal. I'm okay with that. I want you to challenge everything – it adds to the mystery of it all. Bigfoot is still the reigning hide-and-seek champion, aliens are mostly the illegal kind, and ghosts are something that are the topic of campfire stories. I tend to think that the people who call themselves skeptics are that way due to a subconscious fear that they have of the unknown. Or fear that if they announce that they are believers, then the ridicule and odd looks that they will receive aren't worth it.

My goal of writing this book is not to convince anyone that ghosts and little green men are real. My goal is to give others, like myself, the opportunity to read another person's stories, and to possibly give them a slight bit of comfort that what they may have been experiencing is not unique to them. Also, that there are others out there who share the same experiences. Bringing up the subject of ghosts or aliens to family, friends and coworkers is a tough one. It's not usually the topic heard around the water cooler or at Thanksgiving dinner. For some who may be suffering at the hands of a malicious spirit or dark entity, there aren't many places to turn to. People don't want others to know that their home may be haunted.

The world is a very small place thanks to social media, and secrets are much harder to keep these days. That "haunted" home you may be living in might be something that people will actually avoid. Parents might not allow their kids to come over for playtime or birthday parties. For some, they will cast their suspicions on you and think that you are dabbling in non-Christian practices behind closed doors. Also the resale value of your home may actually diminish. I'm not even joking about that one. Believer or nonbeliever, would you purchase a house that the neighbors quietly say is infested with ghosts? And if you actually do reach out to someone at work or confide in friends, you never know how they will react to what you've just told them. Your circle of support might shrink significantly.

Even writing this, I am often tempted to abandon the whole thing and keep all of this to myself. I live in a tight-knit community and certainly am aware of how I may be treated by others if they read this. I will get the polite smiles from friends and family and the awkward grins.

Although, I would like to think that I am prepared for all that. This is a gamble on any kind of reputation that I may have. I have at times walked down the main street of my hometown and have had strangers say, *"Hey, you're the ghost guy!"* I suppose there could be worse things to be known for.

I admit that I will read other paranormal books with my own brand of skepticism. I will read about portals opening with otherworldly creatures crawling out and unseen entities throwing plates across the kitchen and levitating the family dog across the room. I will find myself chuckling and rolling my eyes but suddenly catch myself thinking that even after all the strange things I myself have encountered, how could I possibly think that other people's experiences might be bullshit? I am now in that category of making people roll their eyes and snicker at what a loon I must be. The only crazy thing is that I'm actually putting all this out there for people to either mock or be fascinated by. Hopefully mostly the latter.

I also want to make something perfectly clear, I'm no expert on any of the topics that I talk about. I am still learning, and I know that I have a long ways to go. I'm always seeking out other psychics and mediums, clairvoyants and shamans. I message them and seek out their own vast knowledge. I have found that some are very willing to share their secrets, and some are not. Even though you would think that someone with special gifts would be morally responsible to assist others and give their energy and time without expectation of rewards, this is not always the case. There are hundreds of frauds out there who are more than willing to help you part with your hard-earned money. There are the *"fear-based psychics"* who will prey upon your anxieties and nightmares and actually hype up and exaggerate what is actually going on in your home. The mediums who have a flair for the dramatic and paint a tale of murder and mayhem as they view your property. They have all sorts of sprays and crystals and magical salt to sell you to keep that nasty spirit at bay. Blessed crucifixes and vials of holy water to cast the demons out. Cash or card?

My friend Michelle Desrochers is a very well-known medium who many would recognize from various paranormal shows. She is an expert in her field and tries to assist anyone who may need her help – free of charge. Michelle only goes after demonic and malevolent spirits and travels all over the continent and beyond to help people. She tells me that she has a waiting list that is a year and a half long. She knows that she can't help everyone in a timely fashion, but she still charges full steam ahead. Michelle told me once that charging money for clearing homes is "bad karma", and that no one should take payment for it. That's almost like a firefighter waiting for you to open your wallet before he turns the hose on your burning home. She is a very positive person, a great influence, and I am very glad to know her.

Some "experts" say that we all possess clairvoyant abilities in us, but we have chosen to ignore them or have had them suppressed by others. How many times have you heard of children having imaginary friends or telling you that Grandpa, who passed away not long ago, was sitting on their bed talking with them last night. As adults we write it off as children's imagination and convince them that it's not real. We are pulling the veil down over their eyes as we do, and we don't encourage it, as it's not a societal norm. It would be something that the majority of people would frown upon and try to suppress. Some of us are born with these gifts, and others have to coax them out over time. For me, I am attempting to bring something back to my life that I was forced to suppress as a kid. More on that later.

John, whom you will get to know quite well in this book, is a special case, as his abilities came from out of the blue and weren't something that he sought out or was even interested in. The universe had plans for him, and I am tagging along for the ride. My "veil" is lifting slowly, and my psychic antenna is going further and further up. It's something that I wish that I had pursued decades ago. Who knows where I might be now if I hadn't been told to put it aside.

I have also learned that there are no coincidences in life. I look back at the past two years since joining the paranormal investigation group SHIP (Strange Happenings Investigators of the Paranormal) and think of the incredible things that I have been part of and all the amazing people whom I have become friends with. I would never in my wildest dreams have thought that I would be remote viewing or communicating with spirits. Would never think that I would be assisting in clearing homes of malicious entities or writing a book. Life can be very strange, and things can move very fast. The sequence of events over the past two years has been very tidy in its formation. From the moment that I discovered the *Ghost Adventures* television show, to becoming a member of SHIP, meeting John, starting the podcast (things that you will become familiar with as you read on)...it seems like it was just all meant to be.

Also, just to let you know, some names and very minor details have been changed in respect to people's privacy.

1

BEGINNINGS

My first experience with the paranormal happened to me even before I knew what the word paranormal was. When I was three years old, my parents bought a home in Caledon East, Ontario, Canada, and had moved us out of Rexdale – a subdivision of Toronto. My father had been born and raised in the city close to the old stockyards and saw that his simple city life was forever going to change. It was time for a fresh start, and he and my mom made a conscious decision to get out before the concrete jungle swallowed us whole. Our new home was a small raised bungalow on four acres of land engulfed by farms and forests. Dirt roads with generic concession numbers and side roads surrounded us. A traffic jam in this part of the world was getting a slow-moving farm vehicle in front of you or a deer darting from the bush to scamper to the other side. It was a fantastic place to grow up. The air was clean, the neighbors quiet, and the night sky was filled with stars and the songs of crickets and frogs.

The home had been dubbed by my three-year-old self "Uppa house". My mom would tell me that I would get excited to go see it before we actually moved in, and I had given it that nickname meaning – let's go up to the house! Uppa house.

The home had lain empty for quite some time, so there was lots of work to be done. The grass – all four acres of it – was knee high on an adult, and my poor father had to cut it all with an electric push-mower and miles of extension cord before he acquired a riding lawnmower. I was more than happy to get lost in the tall grass and go on adventures with my dog, Ginger. Those were the days when a young kid could romp around the forests and thickets of a rural setting without the parents fearing the worst. My mom could always find me, as she only had to look for the dog's wagging tail sticking up out of the high grass. There weren't any dangers in the fields or forests that surrounded us for a kid to worry about. There had been another home behind our place, back about four hundred yards, that was surrounded by trees and a nice pond. It had once been a place where nudists would flaunt their birthday suits, and I think a lot more went on back there. Drugs and swingers groups were quite a thing back in the early seventies, and I am certain that the owner of the property made the best of his privacy. They moved out not long after we moved in, and the home lay abandoned for many years. Probably for the best.

It was soon after that things took a turn for "my" worse. I started to have terrible debilitating nightmares not long after moving into the house. These nightmares weren't anything that a young boy's imagination could conjure. They weren't about the boogeyman in the closet or monsters under the bed. No, I would have nightmares about endless fields of rotating gears and cogs clinking and clanking and grinding away. These rust- and brass-colored machines would be turning in terrifying synchronicity. Inevitably, in the nightmare, my father would appear inside the gears, and the machines would tear him apart limb from limb. Pretty heavy and terrifying stuff for a young boy to come up with. I would wake up screaming like a banshee, hyperventilating and confused. My mom would remind me years later that I would always be pointing to an unseen man in the corner of the room who stood there and watched me. These nightmares continued over the years and even into my early teens. Their intensity never faded, but the number of times that I would have them diminished slightly.

I'm not sure when, but my parents found out that the previous owner of the house had committed suicide in the basement of our home. He was a vile abusive drunk and had mistreated his wife and his son. I know his name but won't give him the "honor" of being put into print. Eventually this man's negative and abusive nature caught up with him, and he decided that the world would be a better place without him. He overdosed on pills and alcohol in a small basement bedroom, which was now our music room. The "music room" contained a stand-up piano and my dad's beloved eight-track player. It was connected to the family room, where I spent most of my time watching cartoons and playing with my Star Wars action figures. I would often see a shadow man standing in the door to the music room, watching me. He would enter my peripheral vision, and as soon as I looked straight on, he would quickly disappear. I don't think that I ever told anyone about the shadow person standing in the doorway, and, to be honest, it had never bothered me. I chalked it up to something going on with my eyes or my young imagination and largely ignored it. Life went on, and I would still get that odd terrifying nightmare.

Years later, my mother and her friend Loretta went to a psychic in Toronto for some personal amusement. Before they went, they were instructed by the psychic's wife to bring photos of anyone they wanted him to connect with. My mother took class pictures of my older sister and me. The psychic, whose name I never knew, had apparently been the personal psychic to the late actor Lorne Greene of *Bonanza* and *Battlestar Galactica*. During the course of my mom's reading, the psychic stopped and asked my mother if she knew that we had a ghost in our home. My mother said that she was aware of something odd in our home but hadn't given it too much thought. Over the years, we would hear footsteps on the roof, the washing machine would come on by itself, and the thermostat would move on its own. The psychic then reached over to the upside-down photos that my mom had placed on the table and turned mine over. The ghost, according to the psychic, disliked me quite a bit and focused his negative energy towards me, hence the terrible nightmares. The psychic convinced my mom that this negative spirit would continue to have a negative effect on me, and it was time for him to go.

This was also a period where I was becoming interested in the paranormal and trying to figure out if I had any special abilities. My mother and I made our own homemade Ouija board and would try to connect with deceased family members. My uncle Bud had passed away near this time, and we wanted to connect with him. You will become more acquainted with him later on in the book. Our Ouija board was made of hand-lettered pieces of paper laid out in a circle with a very light wineglass overturned and placed in the middle of the circle. My uncle came through, answering questions that only he would know the answers to, and my mom and I never felt any negative energy come in. People can get quite paranoid about Ouija boards and think that often the spawn of Satan himself is going to come through. I am sure that there are some nasty things that would love nothing more than to use the board to open a gateway of sorts, but we were lucky enough to get family. We always closed the conversation by saying goodbye, and my uncle would always leave with the message – Be good.

As I delved more into the world of ghosts, my psychic

antenna started to go up. I would come to be able to see auras of varying colors around people. I didn't know what they meant at the time and didn't know where or who to turn to but liked the cool colors and left it for what it was. One evening I was sitting on the living room floor, talking to my mom. She was sitting in a chair in front of me, and I was looking at her aura. Suddenly a beautiful blonde "angel" (without the wings) shot upwards through the floor and went straight up into the ceiling and disappeared. I remember that she had a very short white dress on and that she had great legs. *The things that you remember, huh?* She almost seemed to teleport through the room right behind my mom. I never mentioned the gorgeous blonde apparition to her, and this may be the only time I have ever spoken of it to anyone.

The psychic in Toronto finally connected my mother with a lady by the name of Carole Davis. She was a medium who specialized in ridding homes of malevolent spirits. She was a Welsh-born woman who now lived in Canada. She had gained some personal notoriety in the paranormal world and was even the subject of an article in the National Enquirer. She and my mom made arrangements over the phone for her to come to the house to deal with our unwanted spirit. Carole and a gentleman by the name of Ian Currie came to our home one evening soon after the initial call. Mr. Currie was a resident of Guelph and a former university professor who left academe to research the paranormal full time. He often accompanied Carole and assisted her with her house "cleanses". We had no idea what to expect from the two of them and were certainly not prepared for what we would soon witness.

Carole and Ian asked us a series of questions (none of which I can remember) and got a "feel" for the house. Ian told us that when they were on their way to our home, he felt a psychic attack from the spirit while he was driving. Carole had had to do something quickly to remove the negative attachment so that he could focus on driving. He had been overcome with such a strong negative feeling that he said, "Carole, you've gotta get this guy off me!" We all looked at each other and wondered what we had gotten ourselves into. At that time, in the early '80s, there weren't any supernatural or paranormal shows on television (that I knew of). Talk shows might have had the odd psychic as a guest, but the topic remained quite taboo among people and was something you certainly didn't talk about. Now there are endless websites, social media pages, and podcasts on the subject. Lots of places to inform yourself and be more prepared.

I sat across from Carole and Ian in our living room. My parents and my older sister were also in attendance. The spirit, according to Carole and Ian, knew what was going to happen and tried to do anything he could to distract her concentration and focus. Our dog, which was outside on the deck, began to bark incessantly. This is something that was uncharacteristic of the dog, and she would not stop. She barked at nothing at all. My sister had to take the dog and put her in one of the cars out in the driveway to get her to stop. At one point Carole became angry with the spirit and threatened out loud that she would put his soul in one of the cows at the farm across the road. We all looked at each other with puzzled looks. *Was she joking, or could this lady actually do something like that?* Finally it came time for Ms. Davis to perform her "magic".

As Carole sat on the couch in front of me, she closed her eyes and began to breathe steadily and heavily. Within moments she began to almost physically change in front of us. She slouched forward in her seat and seemed to shrivel into herself. Her voice and demeanor changed as she began to channel this spirit and project him. She began to dry retch and started to wring her hands. Her words slurred, and a diatribe of foul language came out of her. She had in essence become the drunken vile man who haunted our home. We all looked at each other in disbelief, as we had no idea as to what was happening and weren't given any sort of heads-up as to what to expect. My father, who was not a big believer in the paranormal, looked like he was going to grab the two of them and throw them out of our house. Mr. Currie just sat there calmly and looked at Carole as if this was something completely normal. I remember him having such a blasé look on his face.

As Ms. Davis "became" the spirit and channeled him, Mr. Currie spoke to her/him. Ian told the spirit that he had to leave the home and to stop tormenting me. He told him to move into the light and move on. He also explained to the spirit that he didn't have a physical body anymore and that it was time to go. Apparently Mr. Currie could see what the spirit was seeing, and there was a bright light with a man standing there to guide the spirit in. The drunken spirit thought that he was in a hospital for some reason and that the man in the light was a doctor. He was confused as to what was happening and apparently didn't know that he was even actually dead. Mr. Currie continued to coax him towards the light while Ms. Davis (wherever she was mentally/spiritually) was doing her part psychically to remove him as well. Mr. Currie continued to speak to the spirit and eventually convinced him to step to the light and be gone once and for all.

Ms. Davis then showed me how to "close my doors". I found out later in life that they were actually my chakras. She explained them to me in a way that a thirteen-year-old would understand. Every night before I went to bed, and every morning when I woke up, I was to perform a quick protection ritual. This was to close myself off from any psychic attack from the abusive spirit, as apparently he could return from wherever they'd sent him, and he could seek me out again. I was also to keep from reading any horror novels or watching any horror movies. According to Ms. Davis, things like that could "open me up" to the spirit again, and he might zero in on me once more. This was something I was to do until I turned twenty-one. It was a heavy blow at the time, as I loved reading Stephen King novels and watching horror movies. But I did it.

One thing that Carole told me before she left was that if the spirit and eventually convinced him to step to the light and be gone once and for all. Moments later, Carole came out of her trancelike state, returned to "normal", and sat up straight. The atmosphere in the home immediately changed. When my father and I stood up, we both felt fantastic. We both felt like a great oppressive weight had been pulled from our shoulders and backs. We both felt ten feet tall and like a million bucks. My mom and my sister didn't mention anything about feeling any different, so it seemed that the spirit was only fixating on the men of the family. It was a sensation that I will never forget and a feeling that I would like to experience again one day.

2

SHIP

S HIP, an acronym for Strange Happenings Investigators of the Paranormal, is a ghost-hunting group based out of Fergus, Ontario. A neighbor of mine had heard that I was interested in the paranormal and told me that a friend of hers, Michelle, was a member of the group. I contacted Michelle, and after texting back and forth for about a week, we finally met face-to-face. Michelle had a great interest in the paranormal, and I listened to her own personal stories. She told me that SHIP had lost a couple of members due to personal reasons, and they were looking to fill some positions. I would be introduced to the team, go on an investigation, and then either be voted in or kicked to the curb. Fair enough – I couldn't wait to go out with them. I wasn't sure what to expect, as the only reference I had for any paranormal investigating was what I saw on television, which was usually groups of people banging around in the dark and shouting, "DID YOU HEAR THAT?!" Regardless, I was excited to go.

Mike C. was the "leader" of the group and invited me to his home along with Michelle and another team member, Barb. They were going to review a large batch of EVPs that they had

captured from a farmhouse that they had investigated a couple
of times. EVPs are electronic voice phenomena. Basically spirit
voices captured on digital recorders. It's believed that ghosts
speak at a different vibrational rate than the living, and the only
way to hear them is with digital recorders. We all sat at Mike's
kitchen table, with our earphones linked in to his computer. We
then reviewed the voices that they'd captured. This was my first
time actually listening to anything like this, and I was excited.
For over an hour we listened to the spirit voices from the
recorders. It was amazing. We heard female spirits talking to
each other in a conversational style. Male spirits and even some
screams from the other side. I needed to know more about this
farmhouse. It seemed to be teeming with spirits. The group told
me that it was a very active location and the family had run-ins
with poltergeist activity, could hear women singing, and much
more phenomena. It wouldn't be long before I had my own
stories to tell from the farmhouse.

Mike C. had made a decision shortly after my first meeting
him to leave the group. He had some personal reasons to leave
and decided to hand over the reins to another team member –
Tony.

Michelle took me to meet Tony not long after in his Rock-
wood home. Tony is a jovial, warmhearted Newfoundlander
who had served with the Canadian Navy for many years. He was
an extremely passionate paranormal investigator and had all the
toys to go along with the hobby. He invited us to his kitchen
table for a drink and some ghostly conversation. Minutes after I
sat down, I saw movement to my left and looked past the kitchen
counter and through an opening that showed the foyer and the
front door. Tony saw my reaction and knew that I had seen
something. Movement from the same area made me look again.
This time, almost in full color, I could see a woman, maybe in
her mid to late sixties, wearing a white shirt and a brown vest,

looking back at me. She had an anxious look on her face and then disappeared as quickly as she had appeared.

"What did you see?" Tony asked. "I know I have spirits in my home," he added. I told him what I saw, and all he had to say at the time was, "Interesting..."

For several hours more, Tony and Michelle had my attention as they spoke of their experiences with the paranormal, some of their more memorable investigations, and other assorted conversation. They were great people, and I hoped to be accepted to the group. It wouldn't take long before I was to join them on an investigation at a lady named Kathy's house.

3

KATHY'S HOUSE

This was my first "real" investigation with the paranormal team. A twenty-year-old home in a regular-looking small-town subdivision. I was disappointed right off the hop. Haunted homes were not supposed to look like this. They were supposed to look like something out of a Stephen King novel. I wanted the Addams family homestead, not a single-car-garage cookie-cutter-style place. Yet, I was to quickly find out that looks can be deceiving.

Michelle and I had gone to Kathy's home about a week prior to the actual investigation to do a preliminary investigation. This consisted of us asking the homeowner a series of questions, having recorders going, and basically trying to get a feel for the place. The main thing is to see if your inner bullshit meter goes off and see if the homeowner is some kind of crackpot or someone looking for attention. Kathy was a single mother of two grown men and apparently had made a lot of poor decisions in life when it came to choosing partners. She seemed non-energetic, depressed, and had had some recent mysterious physical health problems. Not to mention the problems with apparent spirits in her home.

Kathy told us that one of her sons had witnessed a wireless game controller slide off the basement table, she could hear bumping around on the second floor, there was often a strong odor of cigar smoke on the top of the landing on the second floor, and that the dog would go nuts and act uncharacteristically at times. She also said that she often found dimes around the house. Dimes?

If you search the internet and research the link between materializing dimes and their connection to the paranormal, then you will find tons of information and stories from people who find them in odd places around their homes. Kathy even told us that she would be in the bathroom conducting her business and would hear one clink between her feet as she sat on the throne. She then produced a Ziploc bag with about thirty or more dimes to show us her "collection". Spirits, apparently, will drop them around the home when they sense that the owner is under a lot of stress, ill, or in a time of need. I joked and asked if the spirits could drop some hundred-dollar bills instead. As Michelle and I sat on the couch and talked to Kathy, I scanned the floor and furniture, hoping to find a dime. I didn't.

During our preliminary conversation with Kathy, Michelle thought that she heard a disembodied voice in the room and turned to me with a puzzled look. I didn't hear anything at all. She immediately took a cell phone pic in the direction that she thought that it had come from. Later on Michelle looked at the picture that she took. It was amazing to say the least. There, in the pic that she took, was a giant pink swirling mass where nothing else stood in the room. Inside that mass was a light anomaly that looked like a tiny laser beam headed for the roof. Michelle and I were shocked. She had never captured anything like this before. Addams family mansion be damned! Michelle was excited as well, as she had never captured anything like this before.

It was about a week later when the team organized a time for a full and proper investigation. Michelle met me in the driveway of Kathy's home, and we went in and waited for the rest of the team to arrive. Tony and Barb eventually showed up, and we began to unload equipment into the house. Tony took his ghost hunting seriously and had invested a lot of money in equipment. Cases of night-vision cameras, digital recorders, K2 recorders, EMF and Mel Meters, and other assorted gadgets started to fill the kitchen table. I was excited to get my hands on it and use all of the bizarre gadgets. As Tony and I unraveled endless cables and wires to set up some cameras and digital recording equipment, we noticed that there were two dimes on the kitchen table, and I mentioned it to Kathy. She turned from the kitchen counter, where she was preparing tea for everyone, and asked where the dimes had been found. She stated that they were new and hadn't been there before we arrived, as she had cleaned up and they weren't there previously. Into the Ziploc bag they went.

We quickly set up the night-vision cameras. One in the living room, one in the basement, and one in Kathy's bedroom on her nightstand, facing the door. Digital recorders were set up at each camera. We couldn't really do a proper investigation in the basement, as one of the sons was sleeping on the futon down there. It was obviously not the same son who had witnessed the game controller slide off the table, as he'd stated that he would never set foot in the basement alone ever again. Tony set up a "base" at the kitchen table. This was where the cameras were plugged into a digital recorder and a monitor for real-time viewing. There was a problem though...Tony couldn't for the life of him remember the passwords for the system. Without that, the digital recorder wouldn't save anything that we caught on camera. Michelle, Barb and I went upstairs to conduct some EVP sessions while Tony grumbled and cursed at the monitor and his shoddy memory.

We definitely felt a presence in the home. As the three of us sat in a back bedroom, we could all feel the heaviness in the air. As someone who is sensitive to spirits and can definitely feel them clinging to me, I was more than aware of something there. It would crawl up my back at times and ride up and down my right arm. We stayed upstairs for about an hour to conduct EVPs and then retreated to the main floor to see how Tony was doing with the passwords. He sat there at the kitchen table with a slightly perturbed and somewhat frazzled look on his face as he still continued to struggle with the password situation and typed in endless ideas as to what the password might be.

As we took a break, I sat down on the large leather couch in the living room and had set the K2 meter beside me on the end table. On the table was a black metal hanger shaped like Mickey Mouse's head. A round circle with two big ears. The head had metal bars that went across it in order for the owner to hang jewelry on it. Kathy just happened to be a huge Disney fan and had about a dozen Donald and Scrooge McDuck key chains hanging on it. We all sat on the various couches and watched, amused, as Tony cursed and shook his head as he tried in vain to remember the passwords for the recorder. From the corner of my eye I saw the K2 meter light up. There was nothing electronic near it to make it go off. As it went off, the Scrooge McDuck key chain right next to it started to swing back and forth by itself. I alerted everyone in the room to what was happening, and we watched it sway back and forth for a minute or two. None of the other key chains moved. Of course, as we sat and watched in amazement, no one thought to whip out their phones to record it. Amateur move.

Tony gave up on the digital recorder and grabbed the spirit box. The spirit box is something that cycles through AM and FM frequencies at a very high rate of speed. Spirits can use the energy emitted from it and project their voices in real time through it. It can be a very useful tool with one drawback: it makes a hellish noise that no one can really stand for very long. It emits loud static in a pulsing pattern, and it's like nails on a chalkboard. Tony fired it up.

Kathy explained to us that she thought that the spirit that was in the home had been connected to her ex-husband and may have been her ex-father-in-law. Apparently he was a hard-nosed German and had not been the easiest guy to get along with. The spirit box crackled away. Tony asked for the spirits to come forward and identify themselves. He then demanded that the spirit identify itself, and it surprised me that he would make any attempt to antagonize a spirit. It was believed that the spirit had been oppressing Kathy and may have been the cause of some of her physical health symptoms, as her doctors couldn't give her a proper diagnosis.

"I demand you identify yourself," Tony said to the spirit box. No response.

"Speakee dee Dutch?!" Tony said.

Michelle, Barb and I looked at each other and burst out laughing at Tony's attempts to reach out to a possible German spirit in his best Newfie accent. "I think it's 'Sprechen zie Deutsch'," I said to Tony. He started to laugh. "Hablas la Chinese?!" I said to the air around us. Everyone laughed again. Poor Tony. "Speakee dee Dutch" became our unofficial battle cry for the group.

I don't recall any voices coming from the spirit box in the living room. Tony took it upstairs to the bedroom, and I watched him on the still non-recording monitor from the kitchen. As he asked questions (which I couldn't hear from the main floor), I saw several orbs fly around him on the monitor. Orbs are small light anomalies that are believed to be spirits in a certain energy form. Many paranormal investigators – and skeptics – quickly debunk them as dust particles or insects. The thing was, though, that Kathy's house was immaculate. You could eat off the floor of her place. I ruled out dust and insects. Dust doesn't fly through the air and then do a quick U-turn and fly the other way. Also flies and mosquitoes fly in an erratic fashion, and when they get close to the camera, you can see the flutter of their wings. It was also wintertime, and no one had seen an insect in a couple of months. These were definitely orbs, and it was like a Star Wars light show in Kathy's room! Michelle joined me, and we watched amazed as the tiny light anomalies shot around the room like laser beams. Tony eventually left the room and came back down to tell us that he had several intelligent responses from the spirit box.

I picked up a K2 meter and headed for the stairs to go to the bedroom levels. Once at the base of the stairs, something unseen crawled up my back, and I got an icy chill. I let out an audible shudder, which Tony heard and asked from the kitchen if I was OK. I told him that something, or someone, was all over me. I told whatever it was to bugger off and leave me alone as I headed for the top of the stairs. Once at the top of the stairs, I walked right in to a very strong odor of cigar smoke. I called for Tony to quickly join me to verify what I was smelling. As I watched him climb the stairs from the landing, he paused and looked down the stairs behind him. As he did, I was compelled to look in the same direction. We couldn't see anything but were both drawn to look in the same direction. That was the same spot where just moments ago I had felt something trying to attach itself to me. Once at the top of the stairs, I asked Tony to take a whiff. "Cigar smoke!" he said. It sure was, and we could both smell it. Kathy was a nonsmoker, as was her son (still sleeping in the basement), and she stated that none of her neighbors were cigar smokers. None of the windows or doors were open either, as it was wintertime and pretty crisp outside. Tony and I were impressed at the smell. Over the course of the evening, the cigar odor made an appearance a couple more times before fading away again.

Tony and I did some more EVPs in and around the bedrooms and bathroom and then headed for the main floor again. Michelle and Barb traded places with us and went upstairs. As I watched Michelle and Barb conduct their part of the investigation in Kathy's bedroom, I once again watched the orbs fly around the room on the monitor. It was amazing to watch. Tony and I collectively cursed at the failing recorder and pondered as to what the passwords may have been. As I looked at the monitor, an orb shot forward and looked like it went right between Michelle's butt cheeks! I grabbed my phone and texted her upstairs – "An orb just flew up your butt!" I added a goofy-faced emoticon. I watched her on the monitor grab her phone, laugh at the text, and then respond with an "LOL!" Cheeky spirit.

Kathy had told us that she wanted her home clear of whatever was bothering her. Michelle was our resident ghost buster at the time and was proficient in Reiki and using sage to clear out spirits from homes. Michelle walked around the bedroom, making Reiki symbols in the air with her finger and reciting a Reiki protection word. Right after she had done it in the doorway to the room, she headed for the hallway. As I watched on the monitor, an orb shot straight for her. As it hit the threshold of the door frame, it literally put on the brakes, turned, and shot back towards the direction it had come from. It seemed that the Reiki protection had done its job.

Other than the minor poltergeist activity with the moving key chain, the cigar smoke, and the Star Wars orb show, it was a pretty quiet evening. Apparently, according to the others, we hadn't treated it as a real investigation and talked, joked and laughed too much, which would make listening to the recorders a difficult task. I still enjoyed myself and loved every minute of it.

When we conducted the data review of the EVPs at a later date, we did capture several voices, including the grunting of pigs! Everyone seemed a little unsettled at that, but Kathy had stated that her now deceased father-in-law did use to slaughter pigs at some point in his life. We also picked up a woman and little girl's voice reciting her name – Stephanie. Kathy liked to whisper to herself, which threw off the EVPs at times. When we thought that we heard a spirit coming through, we eventually realized it was her talking to herself. Her little huffy dog would often make heavy breathing noises and bark at times as well, causing more confusion when reviewing the digital recorders.

These spirits didn't have any connection to Kathy or to the property and still remain a mystery. Kathy never complained anymore about the strange feelings or sensations in her home, and we never heard from her again. Hopefully she was able to figure out her health woes and is getting rich on collecting dimes.

4

THE TOMB

As an artist (a lazy and easily distracted one at that), I needed to get an office outside the house. There were far too many things at home to pull me away from my drafting table. The bed, my recliner, the couch, the TV, etc...I found a small windowless office in town literally three minutes from home. The rent was cheap, and I was the only tenant in there. The space consisted of three small offices, a bathroom, and a closet. No windows, no distractions. It was behind a local insurance company and only accessible from one rear door. I quickly nicknamed it "the Tomb", and I loved it. There was also a dental office in the next building over, so I had some nice ladies to talk to every once in a while. One of them took pity on my being all alone in there, and she started to bring me some homemade Italian treats. This upset her coworkers, as she never brought them any goodies. I made it a point to rub it in when I could.

Once I set foot in the door, I could feel an undeniable pocket of energy as soon as I stepped in. It was almost like a pulse of energy was surrounding me and running up my back. I asked the landlord if he felt anything when he stepped in the door. He looked at me a little funny and said that he felt fine. I couldn't believe the strong feeling of something there with me. It was almost like a portal that I had to wade through once I stepped through the actual door, and it was always present. I tried to debunk the feeling that I got and tried to reason my way to an explanation. The electrical panel was too far away for me to feel anything from it, and the wall-mounted heating units didn't seem to offer any ideas either. I learned that the building had once been a funeral parlor several years prior. I had no idea what it was previous to that, as it was apparently quite old and one of the original buildings in town.

I quickly figured out that there was definitely something in my office space with me. I often saw dark shapes manifest out of the corner of my eye, smelled an old lady's perfume one evening, and heard knocking on the walls all the time. It turned out that Michelle had practiced Reiki in my exact office a couple of years before when it was a wellness center. She had told me that she smelled the perfume once herself. I often spent late evenings there, so I knew there wasn't anyone in the insurance office up front making any noise. I also knew that an old building made creaks and cracks every once in a while, but these seemed like purposeful knocks. One night as I sat at the drawing table, I felt a cold breeze hit me in the side of the neck. As a windowless office, with only one locked door, I immediately thought that it was something out of the ordinary. I took a pic of the side of my neck with my phone and could see what appeared to be an odd-looking rash there. I immediately texted Michelle and told her what had happened. She messaged me back and marveled at what had happened but didn't offer to run out so late at night to perform her Reiki wizardry (thanks Michelle...)

One evening I left my own digital recorder sitting on a chair in the hallway all night. I was hoping to capture a ghostly voice and prove to myself that there were indeed spirits in there with me. The next night I sat and listened to it. It wasn't long before I sat upright in amazement when I got a very heavy breath right into the recorder. It was an unmistakable sound and sounded like someone purposefully exhaled right into the recorder. I was slightly creeped out but also very excited. I was fairly new to ghost hunting and really wasn't expecting to get anything on what was actually my first solo EVP session. I always had a sense that there was more than one spirit in the office space with me and could often see dark figures move in my peripheral vision. I often also saw little blips of light that would appear in the air, especially in the hallway leading from my office to the front entranceway. I became comfortable with them and treated them as guests. When I would see something manifest in the doorway of my office, I would say hello and invite them in to watch me draw. This would also be the first location that I ever heard a disembodied voice. One late night as I drew in silence, I heard a woman scream to the left of me. It wasn't very loud, but it was unmistakable. I waited for another voice to come, but the air remained silent. I shrugged my shoulders and continued to work on my art.

Tony and Michelle joined me at my office late one night for a mini investigation. The three of us huddled together in the hallway on chairs and sat in the dark with our K2 meters, digital recorders, and the spirit box. We didn't bother setting up any night-vision cameras due to the small confined location. Tony brought out the ever-annoying spirit box and fired it up. We picked up a few responses with the spirit box and even heard a spirit call my name out when we asked whose office it was. We didn't have any success with any spirits touching the K2 on demand though. Listening to our EVPs afterwards, we were able to discern that there were at least five different male voices and two females. One spirit called me a "jerk" and another called

Tony a "bubble-butt". Rude buggers. I had asked the spirits repeatedly to touch the K2 meter and make it light up. This is probably my favorite piece of ghost-hunting equipment. On the recorder you hear me asking several times for a spirit to set it off. In response we got an angry EVP from a spirit clearly replying, *"NO!"* Tony explained to me that often there would be an alpha spirit that kept the others in line. The one who responded with the "NO" was most likely the alpha. One of the EVPs we had recorded was when we were asking the spirits their names. A male spirit came through and said, *"Don't tell them anything."*

One evening when I arrived at my office to do some late night drawing, I opened the door and could clearly see a pair of legs in brown suit pants at the end of the hall, standing outside the bathroom. I hadn't turned the lights on yet, so I was backlit a little from the parking lot lights. As soon as I stepped in, the legs quickly walked into the bathroom and disappeared. I said an audible hello to the shy spirit and continued down the short hallway to my office. He didn't feel the need to reply with a greeting back, so I left him alone.

After our little investigation at my office, the presences started to lighten up, and even the energy at the front door was gone. Tony explained to me that the spirits may have been satisfied that we'd validated their existence with us and may have moved on or were content to be quiet and observe from now on. Eventually, I left the office, as my artwork became more of a hobby as I moved on to other creative pursuits.

5

THE PUB

L iving in a small town, you get to know people, and the local pubs are some of the best places to make new friends and acquaintances. My favorite pub is in an old limestone building right on the river. From talking with a local historian and people who worked there, I learned that the pub had been several things over the years. It had been a tannery, a police station, a VHS rental place, a print shop, an apartment, and more. I also learned that a man had died in the basement about a hundred years ago after falling into a vat of liquid and drowning.

I had asked the manager "Darryl" if we could conduct an investigation there and do some filming for a paranormal documentary idea that I had. He readily agreed and showed some genuine interest even though he professed to being a bit of a skeptic. Some of the servers weren't so keen on knowing what might be lurking in the bowels of the pub though. The pub had three basement areas, and one was called by the staff *"the Gateway to Hell"*. This small basement area was only accessible by a small hatch in the floor, and it was where they stored their summer patio furniture. After looking in, I quickly determined that no one was going in there to investigate due to its cramped conditions.

The time for the investigation came, and the team and I arrived. Accompanying us was my good friend Rob, a writer and director of indie films, his sound tech Jake, and cameraman/director of photography Stephan. The staff and manager finished cleaning the pub, poured themselves a drink, and retreated to the patio to drink and watch us investigate. Some comedian put the *Ghostbusters* theme on the stereo system and blared it throughout the bar and patio as we prepared to set up our equipment. We all had a good laugh.

Talking to the manager, he told me that a week prior to our arrival, almost every evening at around two in the morning, the motion sensor in the bar would go off. He would then be alerted by the monitoring company, leave his apartment, which wasn't too far away, and come investigate the bar for a possible break-in. This had never happened before. He chalked it up to faulty equipment and a coincidence and didn't give it much more thought. One of the head servers, who was a devout skeptic, also had a strange and frightening occurrence happen to him the same week. "Don", who lives above the pub in a small apartment, told me that he was napping on his living room couch. He was woken by an unseen pair of hands that grabbed him around the ankles and gently tried to pull him off the couch. He told me that it had scared him so badly that he'd lain on the couch awake for nearly three hours with his eyes closed before mustering up the courage to look around the apartment. I could see that he was uncomfortable recounting the story to us, which validated it even more for me. Even after having this experience, he said that he remains skeptical of ghosts and haunted locations.

Tony, while driving to the location, had texted his friend John – a clairvoyant of sorts – and told him that we were conducting an investigation that evening. Even without any information given to him, John texted Tony back and asked if we were investigating a pub. He also added that there was an old man who died in the basement about a hundred years ago, and that he was not pleased that we were coming. Perhaps he was showing his displeasure by making the alarm system go off and tormenting poor Don in his upstairs apartment. It became clear to me that the spirits often knew well beforehand that we were coming and would sometimes make a nuisance of themselves.

Night-vision cameras were finally set up around the establishment. One in the basement, one on the back wall facing the dining area and bar, and one in the back seating area. We were good to go. I set myself up with the K2 and a digital recorder in a small alcove between the two dining areas. This was where the staff kept the highchairs for tiny patrons. The K2 was jumping, and I got excited. Tony, being the professional ghost hunter he is, noticed after a few moments that the K2 was going off every six seconds. We determined that there may have been some electrical wires leading to an alarm system that was causing the K2 to pulse. Debunked. Afterwards when I was conducting the data review of the EVPs that I had recorded, I had a bit of a shock. During the K2 going crazy in the vestibule, which we had debunked as an energy pulse from an unknown source, I had still asked if any spirits were with us at the time.

"What's your name?" I asked. A spirit with a thick Scottish accent replied, "Walter." He then added with the same thick accent, "Get out!" What's a ghost hunt without a spirit telling you to get out? Especially a crusty old fart like Walter. Tony joked that you're not considered to be a real paranormal investigator until a spirit had said your name or told you to get out. I had experienced both, so I was pretty happy.

Near the end of our evening, Tony, Michelle and I decided to do some burst EVPs in the basement. Tony took his phone out and set it on a freezer with his voice recorder going. Rob and Stephan were with us, filming. Tony asked a series of questions. Walter the spirit replied, "Open your eyes!" It seems that Walter may have been frustrated and confused as to why we couldn't see him and expressed his concern with that statement. The rest of the night went fairly smoothly other than me almost breaking my ankle and popping a tendon in my right foot as I entered the basement to retrieve one of the night-vision cameras. I envisioned crusty old Walter smirking at that. Whenever I go back to the pub, I always ask the female servers how Walter is doing and if they say hello to him when they enter the basement. I get the rolling of eyes and daggers. I hope they don't mess with my food...

6

JOHN

Most of the stories in this book involve my friend John. After a while you might think that this book is all about him. He plays a big part in my paranormal "adventures" and has almost become a daily part of my life. Since Tony from SHIP introduced us via text messages, there has been maybe a handful of days where we haven't communicated since. We work as a team to move spirits and work and to try to understand what has happened to the two of us so late in our lives. This is his story...

John came to SHIP as a very rattled and on the edge "client". He lives in a small community in Huron County, minutes from Lake Huron. He had contacted Tony through social media and told him that he was experiencing some very strange and very stressful things that were affecting him physically and mentally. He was looking for some answers as to what was happening and was looking for help. John, at the time, had acquired a rental property about twenty minutes from his own home in a much smaller rural farming community. The house needed a lot of work, and John set out to do renovations on his own.

John's first strange happening with the paranormal came

when he was working on the upper floor of the home. He had a bucket on the floor that he threw trash and empty beer cans into. It sat on the floor and off to one corner. When John was in the room working on something, he noticed that the bucket began to shake and move slowly across the floor. John, being a nonbeliever in ghosts and other supernatural oddities, thought that there might have been a mouse inside the bucket and trying to free itself, which made it shake and move. When John checked the bucket, he found that it was only beer cans and garbage inside it. John's logical mind still didn't even go anywhere near the paranormal, and he wrote it off as vibrations from moving trucks going by the house, as it was steps away from the road.

From the bedroom where he worked, he could see into the main bathroom. Something drew his attention to the room and made him turn from the garbage can. As he stood and looked into the doorway of the bathroom, ,he witnessed something completely bizarre. From the top of the vanity, a small nail slid across the counter, levitated in the air in front of him, and then fell to the floor. John, still a total skeptic, didn't have any thoughts or inclination towards the paranormal and didn't flee the room in fear. His analytical mind pondered for a moment, trying to come up with a rational explanation for this oddity. John half expected an actual person to be tucked into the corner of the bathroom, and for a moment he believed he had an intruder. He stepped closer to the bathroom door to try to get a better look. Suddenly, a great gust of wind came at John from the back of the bathroom and enveloped him. It was strong enough to blow some paper blueprints off the top of the vanity and send them flying. Fear kicked in, and John turned and ran for the stairs. As he fled down the stairs, he could feel a strong hand trying to push him down. He managed to keep his footing and fled the house. He never went back alone.

From that time on, something attached itself to John and began to torment him. He would often wake up in the middle of the night after being punched by some unseen force. He also would have something grab his foot and twist it so hard that he would end up waking up and screaming from the pain. This became a regular occurrence, and John began to question his sanity. Also at this time, John began to gain his "psychic" gifts. John had an undetected piece of metal that had entered his shin from a crowbar that he had been using. The metal had created an infection that spread throughout his body and attacked his vital organs. He had come close to death because of this infection, and that was when several mediums and psychics told him that his "veil had been lifted".

John would begin to see spirits and even hear them speak to him at times. This dark spirit that attacked him at the rental property had taken it upon itself to attach itself to him and was the one responsible for the nightly attacks. The entity told John that his name was "John" as well and would often send messages to John that he was going to kill him and could do it at any time. This spirit would be dubbed Big John, as he would project himself as a huge man of about seven feet tall with a massive frame. The torment from Big John became so frequent that John would be afraid to go to sleep at night and would stay up till all hours drinking. He would only sleep from pure exhaustion. The torment continued for quite some time and was wearing John down. He would get threatening messages from Big John constantly, as he always threatened to hurt or kill him. John told me that at one point he would see dark rugby-ball-shaped black objects move across the floor at night when he was wide awake. Once he saw one stop within feet of his home office desk, pulsate in front of him, and then take off like a shot and disappear. John asked the entity Big John what they were. Big John told him that they were his personal "demons" and that they were there to steal John's energy. John's fear turned to anger as Big John continued to torment him. Often John would yell at the threatening spirit and curse him out, hoping that some bravado would get it to leave. He thought that if he didn't show fear, then that might help. It didn't.

One night when John was in his basement, he received another psychic message from Big John. "I could kill you any time I want!" Big John projected to him. John stopped what he was doing and taunted back, "Alright, Big John, you want to kill me. Go ahead. Fucking do it. Show me what you've got!" Moments later John felt an icy hand close around his heart and experienced agonizing pain in his chest. He scrambled out of the basement and headed for upstairs. The pain continued throughout the night, and in the morning, John drove himself to the hospital and checked into the emergency department, thinking that he was having a heart attack. The medical staff hooked John up to a blood pressure cuff and heart monitor and put him in a private area by himself. He continued to have sharp pain and asked for some medication to take the edge off. As the medication entered his system, John became tired and started to drift off to sleep. Then, suddenly, three dark figures in robes entered the room and circled themselves around his bed. John couldn't move. It was as if something had paralyzed him. The call button for the nurse was inches away, but he was unable to even simply move his hand to press the button. John watched in horror as the three figures reached into his chest in the direction of his heart. John's pain quickly subsided, and he felt normal again. The three dark figures disappeared, and he was able to move again. John said nothing to the medical staff about the three hooded figures or what had just happened. They would have checked him into the psych ward for sure. I truly believe, after all the things that I have been told by John and experienced with him, that he actually saw these three beings, and that it wasn't something that was induced by the medication that was given to him. Before long he was cleared by the medical staff and was sent home.

John experienced some other very strange occurrences in his home. One night as he watched TV, he looked over at the chair across from him and saw a small baby-sized green "gremlin"-type creature climbing up the back of a chair. John gawked at it in disbelief and reacted to it by jumping from his chair and almost climbed up the wall to get away from it. The gremlin suddenly became aware that John could see it and met his gaze. Its eyes bugged out of its head in shock, and it quickly vanished into thin air. John said that it looked very surprised that he could see it and that it became invisible as it should have been. It never physically appeared again.

As strange things continued to happen in John's home, he began to leave a recorder on in his bedroom as he slept, in hopes of capturing some of the paranormal activity that he was experiencing. One night he and his partner, Lisa, could hear what sounded like a little person running around the bed. John knew it was the little green gremlin that he'd seen. Neither one of them had the courage to peek over the edge of the bed to look. The next morning John listened to the recorder and found that it had captured the sounds of the little creature's feet as it padded around the foot of the bed. The recorder also captured what sounded like squeaky little grunting noises.

Another evening, John came home to find that his daughters had spilled some face cream on the upstairs hallway floor and had halfheartedly wiped it up, which left a white haze on the floorboards. He left the mess there and made it his intention to tell the girls the next day to clean it up properly. The next morning, John came out of his bedroom and headed towards the bathroom. There, in the white haze, was a child-sized, five-toed footprint that looked as if it had pointed toes and claws at the end of them. John quickly cleaned the footprint up and never scolded the girls for making the mess.

The torment from the Big John entity continued but mostly came in the form of mental projections to John in the way of threatening words. John, looking for help and some insight as to what he was experiencing, contacted a local and respected psychic. The psychic, "Theresa", told John that she had experienced this entity before and that it was well known in the area and had taunted and tormented others as well. While speaking with Theresa, John got the impression that she was fearful of this entity. John had asked her to call him in the near future to help him rid himself of Big John's attachment, but she never returned to his home or called him back. He still hasn't heard from her. John was getting desperate and needed some help from someone.

He contacted another local psychic medium and left an emotional and heartfelt message for her. This psychic, "Keri", told John that she never ever went to clients' homes, but when her daughter listened to the message that he had left, something told her that she had to see him. She could sense that something was very wrong. Keri told John that Big John could only do things to him that he empowered him to do. Big John was feeding off his fear and emotions, and this was giving him the energy to continue to torment him. John said that as he talked with Keri, all of his tension and anxiety faded away. Her demeanor and words filled him with a sense of hope and relaxed him. He hadn't felt this good in a very long time.

Big John continued to visit John at his home and tried to prey on his emotions. This time though, John was prepared and didn't give any reason for Big John to upset him. The entity Big John was huge. He was at least seven feet tall and thick. "A physical specimen," John stated. John said that often Big John would walk past a light and his "presence" was so strong that it would completely block out the light just as a normal living person would. When Big John would do this, John would announce, "OK, good job, Big John. You blocked out the light. Good for you..." This indifferent approach to responding to Big John's visits seemed to work, and Big John's trips to John's home became fewer and fewer, and the threats stopped. Big John still continues to visit every now and then though.

Tony and some of the members of SHIP conducted an investigation of John's rental property. When they met John for the first time at the home, Tony said that he looked like he was suffering from post-traumatic stress disorder. Tony, being an ex-military man, could see the signs. After letting them into the home, John quickly left, as he didn't want to be in or near the home for any length of time. When Tony conducted an EVP session at John's rental property, Big John came through several times. At one point Big John stated through an EVP that he was a beer drinker. Other voices were captured as well that belonged to unidentified men and women. It was a very active home, yet none of the SHIP members had any physical or psychic attacks or attachments.

Tony eventually "introduced" me to John via a text message. John and I texted for quite some time before actually meeting. I had no idea what he looked like, where he lived, or even his last name. One night we decided to test each other's abilities and have a bit of fun. I asked John to focus and try to project to me what his home looked like. I sat back and focused my energy and cleared my mind. A moment later I texted John:

"Gray vinyl." John messaged back and told me to hold on. My phone beeped a minute later, and I looked at a picture of the outside of his home. It was gray vinyl! I was impressed, as was John. Most homes are usually red- or tan-colored brick, even white vinyl. Had I just guessed properly, or had something really happened for us? John later told me that it had taken a lot of

effort and energy for him to project the look of his home to me. I'm just amazed that it had actually worked.

The first time I ever went to John's home, I was surprised at how normal and quiet it appeared. It was on a nice lot surrounded by thick forest and just minutes from the lake. It certainly didn't give any kind of impression that it was a hotbed of spirit activity. I was there for quite some time, and both John and I could see spirits all over the home. They were in the kitchen, the living room, up the stairs leading to the second floor, and on the second floor along the railing. John's second floor is an open concept, and when you walk along the upper hallway, there are rooms to one side and a railing along the other. You can clearly see over the railing and down into the living room and dining area. Spirits loved to walk along the open hall and peer down over the railing. We saw several as I visited. As we sat and talked in his living room, I heard a distinct knocking sound behind my head on the wall. John said that was a normal occurrence in his home, and he didn't give them much attention anymore. John also said that as he talked to me, he could see small little *"explosions of light"* above my head. He said that the spirits were probably checking me out, and that was their way of letting him know.

As John showed me the upstairs area and the spot where he'd seen the clawed footprint in the hallway, we could hear heavy shuffling of feet down below. We stepped from his bedroom and peered over the railing. There on the laminate floorboards were huge water-mark impressions of feet. We couldn't believe what we were seeing. I quickly went down the stairs and put my feet beside the foot marks on the floor. I wear a size 15 shoe, but these footprints were huge. They were at least a size 18 and very wide. They were bare footed and very distinct. It seemed that the Big John entity had apparently come for a visit and made a show of making his presence known. I was holding my digital recorder at the time. "You are a big bloody man, John!" I said.

Later that night when I reviewed my EVPs, a deep man's voice came back and said, "You're right..." When we returned to the living room to talk and enjoy a beer, I looked over at the area where the footprints were. At that moment I could see the spirit Big John in a haze. He was a huge man. Tall and thick. *"A strong-built farm boy,"* I said to John. Big John stood there and looked at me, and I described him to a tee. John confirmed his features and his hairstyle, which was ultrashort and almost down to the wood. The massive spirit then faded away.

John's home was a hotbed for spirit activity, and he told me that they often interfered with electronic devices. True to his statement, my digital recorder only ran for forty minutes, and then I started to have problems with it. I had fresh batteries and should have got hours of use out of the device. Something obviously didn't want me to record any longer and decided to screw with my recorder. John also tried to video record the time that I was there with a GoPro that he had, but something kept turning it off on him even though it was fully charged. In my short forty minutes of digital recording, I picked up twenty-five different EVPs. Some of these EVPs were the absolute clearest ones I have experienced to date. Some of them were complete sentences. A rarity among ghost hunters. John and his home were quite an experience, and I wonder if most of the spirits were connected to the property or connected to him.

THE FOLLOWING IS an original unedited report and some EVPs from Tony's initial preliminary meetup with John and the investigation that took place at the rental home.

～

RIPLEY HOUSE INVESTIGATION

FRIDAY, June 12, 2015
INVESTIGATORS: Tony Harris, Michelle Sarson, Dan Bieman
HOST: John (homeowner)
*(Notes on **GRAY** indicates EVP (Electronic Voice Phenomenon) of particular interest.)*

INTRODUCTION SUMMARY:
ON JUNE 6, I went to Ripley to visit our client John at his house to do a pre investigation. I arrived at the house @ 6 pm, meet the client and after a friendly chat, John told me his story about his paranormal experience in this almost 100 year old home that used to be a general store.

John has two daughters and met a lady that had two daughters, both own homes and as the relationship developed they took turns staying at each others home. John stated that he never felt comfortable staying at his girlfriends place overnight, always waking up in the mid of the night for no reason but felt someone was watching him. Finally, the two decided to move in together and John having the bigger home decided that his place was more suitable for two families to live as one, leaving his girlfriends place for rent.

They had two prior rental parties before the last ones rented the place for a year when suddenly the renters just got up and moved leaving the place in a bad state. Clothes, food, toys and furniture left behind as if they moved out in a panic! A week later, John was able to make contact with the renters (them owing rent) and asked them why they left the place in such a mess? The female ex renter stated "you know why! With all the electrical problems, plumbing not working, light flashing on &

off) and hung up the phone, John was confused and worried that there was electrical / plumbing problems, so he contacted a friend who is a plumber. After thoroughly examining the house, the electrician stated the only thing he saw wrong was moisture near the fuse box in the crawl space, recommending that a dehumidifier be placed there.

So John and his girlfriend started cleaning up the place for the next renters, deciding that a little renovation was in order to enhance the place. John and a friend torn down an existing wall and found a old newspaper lodged between the boards, unfortunately the old newspaper crumbled apart when John tried to take it out. (John regrets not taking a picture before trying to take out the newspaper). This inspired John to place three empty beer cans in the new wall, hoping that 50 years from now, someone will be excited to the cans as he was for the old newspaper! John had just finished sealing the new wall, when suddenly the small garbage can filled with empty beer cans in the kitchen started to rattle! John and his friend both look at rattling garbage can in wonder, trying to figure out why it was rattling! Both concluded that it wasn't a earthquake or a large truck going by (house is next to the main road) but shrugged the event off as a funny incident, not thinking anything more of it.

Two days later, John was in the upstairs of the house alone, just finishing up placing new tiles on the bathroom floor. John had closed all the windows and doors in the house to help dry the adhesive for the tiles. John walked into the adjoining bedroom, looking at his craftsmanship and wiping his hands off with a rag when he noticed through the bathroom door something floating in mid air in the middle of the bathroom! As he gain recognition that something was indeed floating in the air, the object turn towards him, descending slowly to the floor! John walk up to the object, realizing that it was a 10" nail. How could a 10" nail float in mid air? he asked himself, thinking it was a hoax of some kind, he look around the bathroom for string or wire device figuring that someone was playing a trick on him. Noting that there was no devices or wire around, he called out loudly "is there someone in the house?" No reply! John walked around to the other entrance to the bathroom from the hallway, nothing unusual with the exception of the nail on the floor. As he was staring at the nail on the floor, he felt a build up of a wind coming towards him from the sink area and suddenly a great gust wind came towards him sending the paper tile instructions at him with great force. He did felt as if a force of some type passed thru / by him and feeling a sense of anger towards him. John departed the house!

As John was telling me his story in the upstairs bathroom, his whole face was perspiring in a great sweat and his pupils were open as if he was in fear! I ask John if he was ok? And he stated "Tony, you don't understand, this is the first time I have been back upstairs since the incident two weeks ago and I wouldn't be here if you weren't with me"!

John also told me that all his life he has been a atheist and this event has shaken his whole foundation in life. His girlfriend has never had any paranormal experience all her 6-7 years living in this house and even now John told me she is having trouble believing him.

John figures that since the wall incident, the house doesn't like him and wants to know what is in the house and hopefully prove to his girlfriend that he isn't crazy!

On Friday, June 12, WPCI meet up with the homeowner John who open the house to us but refused to stay. The team quickly set up their equipment, deciding to stay as one group to keep the noise contamination down and for safety!

Team set up the **four stationary surveillance cameras.** 1 in the kitchen facing the wall that John had build, 1 in the living room facing the stairway, 1 in the main bedroom facing the bathroom entrance and finally the bathroom facing the sink area. We place **two stationary recorders**, 1 in the kitchen and 1 in the bathroom. (note, now realizing that both recorders were place directly above each other and there is a drainage connection between them, echoing the sounds as if they were in each other rooms). Michelle and Dan **both had recorder** with them. Tony had a full spectrum camera, **SB-11** ghost box and for the first time a **SCD-1** (spirit Communication Device that uses the internet radio waves to act as a ghost box).

INVESTIGATION TIME from 20:17 to 24:52:

0:54 – Don't do that – As Tony tells team that we will do a quick tour of the place!

3:00 – Female sigh, follow by a male calling – Team in the upstairs bathroom tour! Maybe Michelle? (11.0 in clip).

5:06 – Superman? *(male whisper)* - Team moves dresser over to the wall for a clear path. Heard under Tony talking! (0.34 in clip).

8:00 – Anger – Team is moving renovation equipment out of the way in the kitchen. (heard at 6.0 on audio clip).

14:00 – Look around her *(male whisper)* - Team in the kitchen, Tony talking to Michelle about upstairs having a different feeling. (0.12 on audio clip).

27:48 – Get the Girlfriend *(male whisper)* - Tony is laying down the surveillance wire in the kitchen. (0.20 on audio clip). (There is a whisper at 0.12 and 0.32 on this audio clip).

28:37 – Cable Kit – *whisper* - Tony is laying down the surveillance wire.

28:56 – Go ahead, kill him - Tony is laying down the surveillance wire.

34:00 – Fuck You *(male voice)* – Michelle is talking about setting up.

38:47 – Taboo *(male long whisper)*- Team setting up equipment kitchen. (0.15 & 0.30 on audio clip)

41:15 – **My god** – Dan mentions that he is using the facilities.

45:39 – **Can you help me?** - Team is adjusting camera angles, Tony & Michelle in the kitchen, Dan is upstairs.

50:02 – **Can't run on me** – Team is setting up in living for investigation.

53:02 – **Get Out**

7

DUFFERIN COUNTY FARMHOUSE

This was the infamous farmhouse that Michelle and Tony had told me about. The property with the haunted home and haunted barns. Where things really did go bump in the night, and a place where any paranormal investigator would love to get in. A place where EVPs captured conversations, not just a whispered word or two. I was excited to get in there. The team had been there twice before, but this would be my first time there.

The SHIP team arrived at the house in the fall with me now as an official member. It was a beautiful modern-style home with a large extension on the back with two large hobby barns, which held horses and cows. A great view off their back deck showed acres of land connected to a thick evergreen forest in the distance. I learned that the home had once been owned by a Portuguese family, and it seemed that the previous owners had been very aware of paranormal activity as well. During the current owners' renovations, they tore down a basement wall to open up an area. Once the drywall was ripped down, they saw an assortment of crosses inside the wall. An odd but creepy sight for someone to find in their new home. Obviously someone felt the need to add some protection to the home in that particular spot.

The family told the team that the first night that they moved in, something forcibly blew their front door in. They said it was like someone actually kicked the door open. They couldn't blame the weather, as it was a calm night, but they didn't think anything paranormal of it and brushed it off. From that moment on, the paranormal activity in the home eventually began to ramp up, and the family – especially the two kids – were being affected by it. The "kids", actually young adults in their early twenties, had been singled out by the vast array of spirits there and taken advantage of. The daughter, "Casey", went down to the horse barn to shovel the stalls out one evening. It was nice weather, so the horses were out in the field instead of being in their paddocks. Casey entered the barn and headed for the first stall. As she approached the first stall, she noticed from the corner of her eye something dark rush up on her. It was the last thing she remembered. She found herself regaining consciousness on the floor of the barn. An unexplained large red welt was on her face as if something had struck her hard. She would never enter the barn alone again.

The son, "Tim", was tinkering in his workshop in the basement of the home. He was making a mold for something and putting the finishing touches on it. He lost his grip on the mold, and it fell to the floor. Tim went to retrieve it from under his desk but couldn't find it anywhere. He turned the workshop upside down before finally giving up on finding the mold. Approximately a week later, Tim was back downstairs in his workshop working on another piece. From the hallway to his left, he could hear a tink-tink-tink of something coming towards him. As he leaned out from his chair and looked down the hall, he could see the small mold that he had lost coming towards him as if someone threw it down the hall. Tim, trying to be logical, walked down the hall past the mold on the floor and looked for his sister or someone else hiding down the hall and playing a trick on him. The only thing was he forgot that he was the only one home. Tim tore like hell from the basement and fled upstairs to wait for another family member to arrive. It was weeks before he went back to his workshop alone.

One night while the family was at the cottage, the father, "Mike", had stayed home so the livestock could be tended to. In the master bedroom they have a large king-sized bed with a very heavy metal frame. I am a big guy and a fairly strong person, and even I had a hard time lifting the bed frame up by myself. Mike told me that after he had gone to sleep, he was awoken by the bed being lifted and slammed down repeatedly. This happened several times before it stopped. The amount of spiritual energy to do that would be incredible. Mike stayed calm, ignored it, and went back to sleep. Most people would have broken land speed records running from something like that.

Odd things continued to happen in the home. The piano in the front room would play by itself, a woman could be heard singing in the main hallway, and the bed in the guest bedroom often unmade itself. Lamps would be found on the floor where they would have been on a table the night before, and voices could be heard. One of the family dogs began to get physical problems, and veterinarians would scratch their heads, as they couldn't figure out what was wrong. Tony and I turned our thoughts to the paranormal and strongly felt that something dark was affecting the poor animal.

After one of the investigations at the farmhouse, Tony had asked John to remote view the property and see what he might come up with. John could see an older lady in a black period dress scowling at him. She was furious that John could see her, and she shook her fist at him. He picked up on the fact that her grandson was a spirit on the farm as well, and she was looking after him. The boy didn't know how to move on on his own, and the grandmother wouldn't leave his side. After John disconnected from the farm, the old lady visited him at his home a couple of times. Once he saw her in his office doorway, glaring at him and shaking her fist. She even took to shuffling his paperwork on his desk when he left the room and threw a bobby pin at him. Eventually she gave up on John and never came back to his home. John also connected with a young lady spirit who couldn't have been more than twenty-one years old. She had been a school matron back at the turn of the century and had died suddenly at a young age. She was surrounded by spirits of children that she had found and collected to take care of. She was, in a sense, mothering them in the afterlife. John also said there were many other spirits there, but none of them came forward, and they didn't wish to communicate.

Tony and I were eventually able to conduct another investigation at the home. The family was up north for the weekend, and once again Mike stayed back to look after the animals. It was a perfect quiet evening to conduct an investigation. Tony and I arrived around seven p.m., and Mike let us into the home, and we gathered in the kitchen area to talk. As we stood there and spoke, I had a K2 meter in my hand in hopes that something might make it spike. Suddenly, in the hand that I held the device, I felt something gently slap my hand. I told the others what had happened right away. Tony was impressed, but Mike gave me a blank look and didn't have much to say. Oddities in his home were becoming the norm for all of them, and he just chalked this one up as being another.

Tony and I spent most of our time in the main barn, where the horses were held. They were out in the field for the evening, and although we couldn't see them in the pitch black, we could hear them snort every once in a while. We collected some folding chairs and sat down to conduct an EVP session and asked the spirits to connect with us. We did get some EVPs that evening but nothing as epic as the other times that the team had been there. The only EVP that stood out was near the end of the evening when a spirit with what seemed to be a thick Caribbean accent said into the recorder, *"Steel soldier!"* A very weird response.

One time during the night I went into the home and sat in the basement by myself. The home has a beautiful pool table ringed with comfortable chairs. As I sat in the dark with my recorder, I began to ask the spirits to come forward and communicate with me. I didn't sense anything and began to get bored. Across from me on the other side of the pool table were about four or five pool cues leaning against the wall in a bunch. Still holding my recorder, I asked the spirits to move the pool cues for me or to knock them down. After several minutes of asking and getting no response, I gave up and headed back to the barn. Later on when I reviewed my recordings, I heard the strangest thing – *the sound of pool cues being moved!* I have spent a lot of time in pool halls over the years and know the distinct sound that pool cues make when you clack them together. This was an undeniable sound. The cues hadn't budged in the basement, but on my recorder, I could hear them being moved around. It was almost as if in the spirits' reality, they were moving them and making the noise, but in my reality they were absolutely still.

Tony and I went back to the farmhouse a couple of weeks later to present all of our EVP evidence to the family. We stood in the kitchen and waited while Tony set up his laptop to a speaker so he could play the EVPs for all to hear. As I stood with my right side leaning against the door frame to the kitchen, I noticed something from the corner of my eye. As I turned to look, I could see a very clear apparition of a beautiful young woman. She had short blonde hair and was of average height and build. She was so clear that I could see her eyelashes. She looked at me with a bit of curiosity and extended her neck to get a better look at me. I smiled back at her and kept eye contact. She then drifted back down the hallway and out of sight. Her apparition was so clear and vivid that it gave me chills. I let out an audible shudder, and everyone in the kitchen looked at me. I told them what I had just witnessed. I concluded that this was the spirit of the schoolteacher that John had viewed, and I was excited that she had allowed me to see her. Tony and I presented the evidence to the family, and the rest of the night was uneventful.

The next evening at my home I was watching television in my living room. I could see something move from the corner of my eye where my living room connects to the dining room. I knew there was a spirit there but couldn't figure out who or what it was. I took a picture of the spot and sent it to John via text. John told me that he got the impression of a woman, and there was a young boy with her, but he was on his knees and hiding under the dining table. It suddenly came to me! *It was the school-teacher from the farm with one of the kids!* Just then I could see several blond-haired kids running around my living room as if they were playing tag. Something that little kids would actually do. As I watched these little blips of fast-moving spirit kids run around my room, I looked over to the other couch, where my dog was sleeping. As I looked at him, I could see the tassels of his blanket, which was hanging over the edge of the couch, swaying back and forth. I was even able to catch it on video and showed John and SHIP at a later date. It was as if one of the kids was on his or her knees and right in the dog's face as he tried to sleep. Then my dog got up, looked perturbed, and moved to the other side of the couch, something that he had never ever done before, as he knew he would get in trouble for being off his blanket. The schoolteacher and the kids visited for a few more minutes, then left. I imagined that she had followed me home to see what I was all about and to make sure that I wasn't a problem for her or the spirits of the kids.

The next day after tinkering on the lawn and in the garage, I decided to go to the basement for a nap on the couch. I dozed off quickly and maybe slept for about an hour. As I began to wake up and slide my legs off the couch, I saw a woman's hand manifest in front of me. It was connected to an arm wearing a black dress. I couldn't see anything else other than a bony fist come flying at my face. My head snapped back as the fist connected with my upper lip. The resounding sound of the smack and the jolt of the punch had me wide awake and alert. The old lady from the farmhouse had just bashed me one! I could taste blood in my mouth, and I quickly jogged to the bathroom to check. I rinsed my mouth out and spit in the sink. No blood. It was odd. I could taste the metallic tang of blood in my mouth, but there wasn't any. It was as if in her reality she had cut me with the punch in the mouth, but in my reality there wasn't anything there. I was so excited. *A ghost had punched me in the face!* It didn't scare me or intimidate me at all. This was going to be an exciting story for the members of SHIP. When I told John, he called me an idiot and said that only I could get excited about being popped in the mouth by a spirit. He had taken more than enough shots from the Big John spirit and wasn't happy about any of them.

That night John and I were communicating via text messages about the farmhouse. As we "spoke", I kept getting the numbers 4-8-9-1 in my head over and over. I told John about it, and he told me to hold on. He texted me back and said that I had the numbers right but in the wrong order. It was the old lady spirit that was trying to project the year 1894 to me. John began to connect to her and received messages. 1894 was the year that she had passed away. He messaged me that she wouldn't leave the farm because her grandson's spirit was still there, and she wouldn't abandon him. She then began to cry to John and said that the reason why she had attacked Casey and me was that she felt that anyone with any psychic ability was a threat to her and might make her leave the property unwillingly. She promised John that she wouldn't hurt anyone again if they promised not to interfere with her presence at the farm. We agreed. Even though it was exciting for me to be struck by a spirit, I didn't necessarily want to go through it again. SHIP hasn't been invited back to the home yet for any more investigations, but I certainly hope they call us back one day.

8

CLIFFORD HOUSE

Clifford is a small rural town in a farming community in Southwestern Ontario. Tony received a call from a very rattled and frightened couple from a small brick rental home there. The couple, Melissa and Joe, stated that they had moved into the home in June of 2017 and by September were ready to move out. Apparently a malicious and mischievous spirit was inhabiting the home with them and was hell-bent on making things uncomfortable. Joe told Tony that they heard banging coming from the basement, footsteps from inside a small closet, cupboards in the kitchen would open and close, and chairs moved on their own. Joe also stated that he often woke up with scratch marks on his ankles and calves. Melissa told Tony that she could also see a shadow man in the living room quite often. The feeling of something in their bedroom was so heavy that it prompted them to pull the mattresses out and sleep on the living room floor.

One morning after their son had gone off to school, Joe decided to take a video on his cell phone. He had mentioned the weird occurrences in his home and was most likely met with skepticism and scoffed at. He wanted everyone to know that what he and Melissa were going through was absolutely real, and he would prove it. He stood in the kitchen and pointed the camera at the cupboards. Joe then asked the spirit in the home to open one of the cupboards. He stated out loud that no one believed him, and he wanted some proof.

Moments later, a small shimmering light anomaly can be seen leaving the window area of the kitchen and shooting towards a cupboard. Seconds later it opens on its own. You can clearly hear the fear and surprise in Joe's voice after he witnesses this.

Tony visited the house one morning for his preliminary investigation. He asked his usual questions, kept his digital recorder going, and walked the home and property. He spoke with Joe and Melissa for a while in their kitchen, where everything was quiet and normal. The three of them then stepped outside to talk for a while. A half hour later, the three of them entered the kitchen again, only to find that one of the kitchen chairs had decided to move itself from under the table and slide over against the counter.

John was asked to do some remote viewing of the home and the property. Tony sent him pictures and the video of the cupboard. The shimmering light anomaly from the video was what John used to connect with the spirit in the home. It was a male spirit. John figured out that he had passed on in his early to mid forties, was a short person, and had some obsessive-compulsive traits that caused him to take his anxiety out on the couple in the home. There were some odd construction quirks in the home that bothered this spirit so much that he actually obsessed about them in the afterlife. The funny thing is that it wasn't even his home, and he had never lived there. John believed that the spirit had taken a shine to Melissa after seeing her somewhere else and had attached himself to her and followed her home. He was jealous of Joe for having her, the home, and everything else that he never had in life. This was also a time when I myself was trying to make some sense of any intuitive or psychic abilities that I may have. Tony believed that I had some abilities and had connected me with John to see what the two of us could figure out together. For weeks John and I had texted each other well before actually meeting face-to-face or talking on the phone. As I stated previously, I didn't even know what John looked like, and at the time of writing this, I still didn't even know his last name. John asked me to focus on the home and the spirit and let him know what I could pick up. I had yet to visit the Clifford home yet.

I lay down and made myself as comfortable as possible and focused on the home. In my mind I could see a four-pane window and a circle inside a square. I had no idea what any of this meant. The images came to me like they were drawn in dull white chalk on a blackboard. I texted John about the window and the circle inside the square. As I did, it dawned on me! The circle inside the square was some sort of vent. John agreed. He received flash images and confirmation from his spirit guides that I was right about this. John had already previously had images of the window and a vent and was excited that the two of us were getting the same images. I myself was shocked and a little impressed with myself. This was life changing for me.

We tried some more, still texting each other and sharing thoughts on the house and the spirit inside. I got the impression that the spirit's name started with an R. Yes, John confirmed with me from his spirit guides that this was correct. We started calling him Raymond after that. While trying to connect with the spirit, I noticed that my throat started to burn and get really sore. I texted John and stated that I believed that the spirit had been a heavy smoker and died from throat-related issues. *Probably cancer,* I texted. John confirmed I was right again. I also got the impression that the spirit had a Portuguese or Italian background and worked with his hands. John received the same feelings. John believed that the spirit had worked with wood and/or chemicals when he was alive. This was possibly why some of the minor construction quirks in the house bothered him so much.

A few days later Tony and I visited the Clifford house. John met us there, and we physically met for the first time. We both mentioned that our GPSes weren't acting properly on the way to the home, and we were getting turned around. John stated that his GPS had told him that he had another thirteen kilometers to go, and the only way he didn't drive right past the house was that he'd glanced over as he passed it and connected that that was the place. We decided that the spirit wasn't happy with our attending and tried to throw us off by interfering with the GPS.

Tony, John and I met with Joe and Melissa outside in their garage. Joe was fidgety and nervous as hell. We could tell that the spirit was feeding off his emotions, and this was what he was using to charge himself on. Melissa was much more calm, but you could still sense that she was uncomfortable and had some anxiety as well. We all talked about the occurrences in the home and our thoughts about what was going on inside the place. After a few minutes we all went inside. Tony had already been to the home, John had been here astrally, as he'd remote viewed it before coming, and I was seeing the inside for the first time. As soon as I entered the home, I stepped into the kitchen and saw a shadow figure standing in the living room. It quickly vanished, and I let the others know what I saw. Tony did some base readings with his temperature gun and Mel Meter, and John and I tried to get a feel for the place. All of us went down to the basement. As this home was a rental, Joe and Melissa didn't have a lot of furnishings. The basement was completely bare. No furniture at all. A family room, small bedroom and a large unfinished furnace room, which had firewood scattered on one side of the room and a large wooden cabinet sitting off to the other. As soon as I walked into the furnace/wood room, I saw it...

The circle inside the square! The one that I had envisioned in my mind. It was a clean air filtration system hanging from the ceiling. It looked like it was brand new and had never been used. Its cord hung from one side of the unit and dangled in the air. A circular end cap stared right at me. John and I determined that the fact that this expensive piece of equipment was installed but not operational was making the spirit's OCD kick in, and it bothered the hell out of him. He had projected his disgust over this to John and me. Joe pointed out that the cabinet in the room had a drawer that he often found open even after closing and latching it. I looked inside and found some manuals for the furnace inside it. We had a strong feeling that the spirit was trying to get Joe's attention to the manuals to make sure things ran smoothly in the home with the furnace and the clean air system. This made Joe emotional, and he began to get charged up. John warned Joe that this was what the spirit wanted. His getting emotional over the spirit's "actions" were what the ghost was feeding off of. John knew quite well the dangers of letting a spirit feed off emotions.

Upstairs in the kitchen, Melissa had told us that she'd confided in an aunt about the strange happenings in their home. The aunt had acquired a small vial of holy water from somewhere and told Melissa to sprinkle it around the house. After sprinkling the holy water around the house, Melissa set the bottle on top of her fridge. When she came out later on, she found the bottle on top of the garbage can. Clearly a message from the spirit telling her what he thought of her holy water. Melissa's intentions weren't strong enough for her belief in the holy water, and it had failed. Her anxiety and fear of the situation were stronger than her motivation.

Also on the property was a large barn with a garage/workshop. Inside the barn, Melissa had a liquidation business where run-offs of merchandise could be found piled on tables, racks, and on the floor for arranging. Joe's workshop was connected to it. As soon as I stepped into the barn, I saw the four-pane window. The same one from my vision. It was high up above a small loft at the far end of the structure.

Tony walked around the barn with his digital recorder. He stopped in one corner and turned to us with a bewildered look. *"I just got told to fuck off!"* he said. Tony has a very keen sense of hearing and often hears disembodied voices when no one else can. When he listened to his EVP afterwards, you can faintly hear the spirit tell him to "fuck off". John then looked to the door where we had all entered the barn from the workshop. "There he is!" he exclaimed, pointing at the door. John saw the male spirit in an almost full apparition, looking at him from the workshop into the barn. John quickly made his way towards him, and I quickly followed. Joe and Melissa stood frozen and looked like they wanted to take off. John and I sensed that the spirit retreated for the safety of the house again.

John asked me to stay in the barn as they all went back to the house. He wanted me to stay in case the ghost decided to head back here and flee from him. Moments after everyone left, I quickly felt an energy come up behind me and cling to my back. "No touching!" I said. "Get off me. You are not allowed to touch me. Bugger off!" The energy dissipated as quickly as it came. I stayed in the barn for about five minutes and then decided to return to the house. As soon as I entered the side door from the garage, I could hear commotion from the basement. When you enter the side door, you can see straight down into the basement down the stairs. Joe and Melissa stood at the base of the steps and were huddled together. Joe was beside himself and reacting in his emotional way. "You should have been here about one minute ago!" he said, looking up the stairs at me. "That thing just booted that box over in the corner!" John confirmed that the spirit had gone over to the corner of the room and violently kicked a large cardboard box that sat on the floor against the wall. I had just missed it. I was so disappointed! This spirit was acting out and behaving like a little kid. He was so despondent that John was chasing him around the property that he lashed out like someone with a short fuse would. Tony was in the furnace room with his recorder, and when he played it back, you could clearly hear the box get kicked with some force in the other room. John had a smile on his face and said that it was pretty cool to see the box get smoked. I was glad that John, who had previously gone through so much turmoil with his malicious poltergeist, was so cool and collected now. He had certainly overcome any fears of the unknown and was now showing a confidence that radiated to the others around him.

For another ten minutes or so, John chased the spirit around the basement with a K2 meter. He finally got the spirit to stop and began to ask him questions and to use the K2 to respond with yes and no answers. Often we ask spirits to use their energy and use the K2 to communicate with us. It's a small plastic device about the size of a TV remote and has six small lights at the end that start from green to yellow to red. John asked the spirit to use the K2 to respond. A small light burst to green for "yes" and all the way to red for "no". The problem was that the spirit didn't like the questions he was being asked. John asked him why he felt obliged to stay in a house that he didn't have any prior connection to, and why he was being a bully to others when he was most likely bullied when he was alive. John and I sensed that the spirit retreated to the barn again to pout.

We all moved back to the main floor and gathered in the kitchen and living room. I noticed that a sectional couch that I had been sitting on earlier had a piece that had moved substantially since we were in the home earlier. I pointed this out to Joe, who didn't even want to look in the direction of the couch, and he fled for the kitchen. We gathered at the kitchen table for a drink of water and to think about what to do about this spirit.

From where I was seated, I could see down the hallway towards the bedrooms. Looking back at me were the spirits of three old ladies standing in a row. They were kind of huddled together, looking at me with curiosity. I told John what I was seeing, and he confirmed that there were three of them without even looking down the hall. I asked the ladies to come forward and talk with us, but they wouldn't budge. They were talking among themselves and kept eye contact with me. After a few moments they disappeared. John had an idea that they headed for the back bedroom, which was the son's room. He took the K2 meter and headed back there. "Yup, they're back here in the bedroom," he shouted down the hall. John had a strong feeling that one of the older ladies was a former owner of the home and that she was delighted that there was a young couple with a son enjoying (or trying to enjoy) her former home. The elderly lady spirit wanted them to make their mark on the home. Unfortunately, "Raymond" had other plans for them.

It was getting close to the time that the son would arrive from school, and we wanted to get out of there before we had to explain to him why three strange men were in his house with all this strange-looking gear. Joe also had to leave for work for his afternoon shift. We said our goodbyes, and John told Melissa that he believed that the spirit would hole up in the barn for the evening. We advised them to go to a shop in Fergus where they could purchase some sage and do a cleansing of the house. We all actually secretly hoped that the spirit didn't do something to Melissa that evening when Joe was away at work. I got the impression that the spirit actually was crushing on her and wouldn't do anything to scare her. He was more interested in making Joe a frazzled mess.

About a week later, Melissa secured some white sage from the Fergus shop and asked John to come back to the home to help her cleanse it, and rid the home of Raymond. Apparently Raymond had decided that Joe and Melissa weren't reacting to his ghostly bullshit like they had previously, and started to terrorize their ten-year-old son. One night after going to bed, the son came flying out, stating that he had seen a shadow man in his room, and it had talked to him. The bully strikes again.

The morning that John was to go to the house, he sent me a picture and a text. It was a picture of his left ear and jaw. You could see three little bloody puncture marks. One on his earlobe and the other two right next to the ear where it meets the jaw. The text read:

Someone really doesn't want me to come cleanse the house!

John arrived and took Melissa around the home, burning the sage and telling Raymond to leave the property and to never return. John told me later on that the spirit pleaded with him and asked him not to do this. The spirit didn't want to leave and had nowhere to go. His parents had been deceased for some time, but they weren't waiting for him or calling him to the light. He believed that they were in Hell, and if he entered the light, then that's where he was likely to end up as well. John didn't listen to his nonsense and rid the home and property of him. The atmosphere changed in the home, and the air felt lighter. Raymond never returned, and the family are enjoying their home.

Shortly after we completed our investigation and John rid the home of the spirit, I saw online that there was a reality-based television show that was looking for people's personal ghost stories. I contacted the show and told them about the Clifford home. I was contacted very quickly by one of the producers and told him the entire story of what had happened. I gave them Melissa and Joe's information, and they were more than happy to tell their story on TV. A day was set up where all of us would be interviewed for the show and tell the audience of our involvement and experiences at the home. The hours of interviews would then be heavily edited for the fifteen-minute segment that would be televised, and actors would reenact some of the actual occurrences.

The show aired several months later, and I was excited to see my mug on the tube and see how they reenacted everything. I found myself rolling my eyes and laughing at some of the reenacted bits. The person who played Tony was some skinny twenty-three-year-old kid, and the guy who played me was a hipster-looking guy with a big bushy beard. The best part though was the way that they portrayed the spirit Raymond. When John and I viewed Raymond, he was a short, chubby, nerdy-looking guy with glasses and regular clothes. In the show he was portrayed as being a menacing black hooded pasty-faced ghoul that bared his fangs at all of us as he "floated" around the house. *That's Hollywood for you!*

9

SALEM FARMHOUSE

I had joined a community Facebook page and had posted that SHIP and I were looking for new hot spots to investigate. I had a lot of success and received several responses from people in and around the area who wanted to share their own ghost stories. One such person was "Lana". She grew up in a beautiful old farmhouse located outside Salem, Ontario. Lana told me that her parents still owned the house, but had built another one on the same property, and the old one was slated for demolition. Its years had caught up to it, and its structural integrity was wearing thin. Lana told me that they had always thought their home was haunted, as they had some strange occurrences over the years that they couldn't explain. The kitchen faucet came on by itself, exercise machines' heart rate monitors would pulse on their own, and Lana always thought that there was a strong uncomfortable presence in the main living area. The home also had a dark history with one of the families that had lived there previously. Apparently a woman was beaten into a coma on the property. The assailant's guilt consumed him, and he took his own life in the barn by shooting himself. You can still see the bullet hole in one of the boards from where it exited his head. A medium friend of mine had gone to the home once by request from the family, and as she toured the place, she received a strong feeling that she should avoid the back of the upstairs rooms. She couldn't give a distinct answer for feeling so uncomfortable with the spot but avoided it like the plague. This investigation was to be a short one. My friend Rob and I were to do some more filming and brought along a young guy named Jake to take care of the sound and another friend of Rob's by the name of Katelyn to work the camera. Tony came with us, as he was still the only one who owned any actual ghost-hunting equipment, and it was hard to keep him away from a good ghost hunt. We arrived at the home and were met by Lana's mother. There was an event going on in the workshop/man cave, where the men of the family had returned from a successful hunting trip and had harvested a moose and bear. We took a quick tour of the home, and it was completely empty of furnishings, and most of the fixtures had been taken down as well. Only a few lights remained. Lana's mother cautioned us to be careful, as all the metal heating grates had been removed from the floors, and only thin planks of wood covered the holes to ensure that no one stepped in one and broke an ankle.

Soon we were unpacking equipment and preparing for our investigation. Rob and I walked into the dark living area to survey the room when we heard a sharp but quick scraping sound from behind us. We turned quickly but didn't see anything out of the ordinary. We started moving some of the fixtures that had been taken down that were now resting on the floor, to try to replicate the noise we heard. It was obvious that something had moved; we just couldn't figure out what. I stepped past the living room and into the hallway that led from the main entrance. When I looked down, I noted that one of the boards that had been covering the now removed grates had been "kicked" by some unseen force and was now several feet down the hall and exposing the open hole. Rob and I were very excited but also disappointed. We lamented that the spirits just couldn't have waited a few more minutes before moving objects. We hadn't unpacked the cameras yet and didn't even have a digital recorder going.

Several minutes later we finally got fully prepared and were ready to investigate. Rob and I worked our way through the house with a K2 and our digital recorders. Katelyn kept up the rear and filmed us with the DSLR camera while Jake sat in the kitchen and monitored our mics for sound. We didn't get any hits on the K2 or any other poltergeist activity. The spirit box produced some male and female voices but nothing that was clear enough for us to make out. Then Rob asked the ghosts if the noise of the irritating spirit box disturbed them; a female voice replied, *"Maybe..."* We all chuckled over that.

Down in the living room, there was a mattress leaning on the wall, and I assumed that it was to be removed to go to the other house. Lana's mom had joked that we could have a nap if we wanted. My back was sore for some reason, so I actually put the mattress on the floor and lay down to stretch out. Tony was in the dining room, which was connected to the living room. His keen ears caught something as usual. "I just heard something tell us to get out!" he said. Sure enough, when I reviewed my digital recorder afterwards, you can hear a male voice tell us to get out. It repeats itself two more times but is only heard on the digital recorder for the other two times. One thing that is rare in our investigations is to get a spirit to give us its name. On Tony's recorder you can hear me ask for a name, and in reply we got the response, *"Dave Wilson."* It was quite clear and a class A EVP.

The rest of the investigation went on without a hitch and not much more paranormal evidence. The home has since been torn down, and I often wonder where the spirits went from there.

10

THE GREYS AND THE OAKVILLE HOUSE

Tony received a call from a woman from Oakville, Ontario. Oakville is about a half hour west of Toronto and rests on the shores of Lake Ontario. The woman explained to Tony that she lived in the basement apartment of a home with her young five-year-old son and husband. She stated that there was some odd activity in the apartment, and it was making her uncomfortable. She often would hear whispering voices, light knocking on the walls, and once witnessed the window blinds move on their own. She also reported that she saw an image of a child and woman. This is the initial email from Maria – **Without edits...**

My name is Maria, i'm from Portugal, we've been living in Oakville since 2014. I grew up in a house that had a lot of paranormal activity, so i always been very sensitive this matter.

We've been living in this basement apartment for 2 years now and never had any activity, but for the last 3/4 weeks i started to feel something is there. Our 5 year old son started to be scared to be in his room, he says he sees things moving and saw a all white figure. This past week, i noticed his room very cold, so two days ago i smudged the house like usual but this time when i tried to light up the sage it would just extinguish. I felt like it didn't want me to do it. And after some minor disturbances around the house, last night my son ran to our room, you could see the fear in his face, as soon as he laid down in our bed, me and my husband heard, "Wanna Play?"

I feel that whatever it is means no harm but it's scaring my little boy. A similar situation happen back in Portugal when my son was just a baby but i had a spiritual guide and a priest who helped us. Now we're alone here, i don't know anyone and i don't know what else to do.

Tony conducted a preliminary investigation of the apartment and as usual took along his recorder and camera. He took several pictures of the little boy's room, as there had been some substantial odd activity in there. Tony sent several pictures of the boy's room to John and me and asked us to see what we could pick up on. I settled into my chair and concentrated on the pictures before closing my eyes. At once, I saw an image of a very large and very tall shadow man standing at the top of a staircase. He noted my presence and retreated quickly down the hall and out of view. He was huge, like Bigfoot huge. I am six feet seven and know that if I had stood next to this apparition, he would have towered over me. I kept my eyes closed and continued to focus on the kid's room. My mind's eye went completely black, and for a moment, I was picking up a pulsing sensation of energy waves emitting from the boy's room. Then three familiar-looking faces pushed forward out of the black towards me. I instantly recognized them. Grey aliens! These beings were popular among UFO and alien enthusiasts and conspiracy theorists alike. We have all seen them on popular sci-fi shows, and the internet is host to hundreds of sites dedicated to them. Ghosts were one thing for me but aliens? This was a bit much. For a brief moment I wondered if my own fantastic imagination had taken over. The Greys looked at me for a brief moment and seemed almost annoyed with my remote view of them. Then they quickly drew their energy back and faded away.

I sat in my chair for a couple of minutes and pondered whether or not to tell John what I had picked up on. He would think I was nuts, I thought. I was curious as to what he'd picked up on though. After Googling an image of a Grey and saving it in my photos app, I sent him a text...

Me – This is going to sound crazy, but I kept getting images of this...[I inserted an alien Grey pic that I found on Google]

John – F me! Hold on

Seconds later John sent me a picture that he had hand drawn after remote viewing the Oakville house. It was a picture of two very tall alien Greys wearing robes with hoods around their heads. *Holy shit!* There was no way that John could have drawn that picture in a matter of seconds, taken a pic of it with his phone, and then sent it to me. His next text revealed that he had sent it to Tony that morning, so he was ahead of me with his viewing of the home. This was legit. I texted Tony the same pic that I had sent John as way of explanation as to what I'd picked up. He sent me a message back saying that I was a funny guy and I had already talked to John and had set this up. He was taken aback when I flat out told him on my kids' lives that I had remote viewed the same things as John on my own. Tony was beside himself and freaking out a little. "Holy shit, what a team we are developing," he texted. He messaged John just to confirm that we weren't pulling his leg and continued with his excitement. The thing was that John saw a very different type of Grey than I did. His were unbelievably tall and wore robes with hoods. The ones that I saw were the classic naked guys who stood about four feet tall. I wasn't even aware that there were tall ones. This was something that I would have to look into more. When I did research it a little more, I learned that there were three types of Greys. There were the generic little guys that I saw, some taller ones that are around six feet, and then these massive NBA-height ones with dark robes. Thank God for the internet!

Over the next couple of days John and I kept in touch and messaged each other many times in regard to what we had experienced. John told me that since he had remote viewed the tall Greys, they were now visiting him at his home. He sent me a pic one night of a mist that had formed in his living room. He took another pic moments later and sent it to me. In the pic you could faintly see the two tall Greys wearing their hooded robes and standing in John's living room, looking at him. They were barely visible and almost completely transparent.

A couple more days went by, and we kept watch for any more *Close Encounters*. While watching television in my living room one night, I caught a very faint apparition of a small four-foot Grey watching me from my dining room. I looked back at "him" and waited to see what would happen. He stood there for a few moments, staring with his huge black eyes, before fading away. I went back to watching TV.

John messaged me and told me that he was continuing to get visits from the hooded Greys. He also told me that the shorter of the two (which was still over seven feet tall) had an amazing ability to rob people of energy. John explained that he'd had company over on the weekend when the shorter one showed up once again. It had drained everyone except John of their energy, and all his guests ended up falling asleep in their chairs. Even the pets crashed.

One of John's spirit guides told him that the door of the little boy's room back in Oakville was an energy portal and that it was a way for the Greys and spirits to travel back and forth. One thing that I had forgotten to mention to him was that I had picked up an image of a regular-sized door with a bright light emanating from behind it. The light poured out from the seams around the door in my vision. We were validating things once again. The weirdness continued, and John explained to me that when he went to bed, he hoped to dream of the Greys. When he did, his guide told him he would be surrounded by dime-sized bright green orbs and that they were there for his protection from whatever was manifesting in the kid's closet. We never officially decided not to tell Maria what we had picked up in her home but kept it to ourselves anyways. I am sure that her strong Catholic upbringing would be put to the ultimate test if she was told that E.T. was using her son's closet to travel between worlds. Like I said, ghosts were one thing, aliens another. Yet Tony received another email from her, which made us sit up and take even more notice...

Hi Tony,

Very interesting indeed, and scary. There are days that i don't feel anything, it almost makes me believe there's nothing there, that it's all in my head but then something happens that i can't explain.

What happened in my bedroom scared me, I shut the blinds and when a turn i heard something, i looked and the blind opened on my husbands side, like when you're peaking, it was so fast, i just closed the bedroom door and run. Then i went there and said something like "who ever you are just stop, you're scaring us". I haven't heard anything until Tuesday, all that knocking, like it just wanted me to get up.

Also i didn't tell before but my husband says that maybe i should, i just don't want to sound crazy.

Sometimes i have like visions, when i close my eyes at night, even when i wake up like at 3/4 am and try to sleep again, i see like human figures but all dark, i've seen a child, a young woman and last one was like a man but, i know it sounds crazy, he's face was like an owl face black and white with deep black eyes. I don't know what to think.

Thanks Tony,

Maria

"An owl face black and white with deep black eyes." Well, John and I suddenly didn't feel so strange after all. Maria had definitely seen what was no doubt a Grey.

John had many more visits by the super-tall Greys at his place and was starting to get annoyed with them. They would appear in his living room, usually when he was trying to relax in front of the television, and they just stood and stared at him. He even came to the point of telling them to fuck off. They didn't offer any communication at all – just stood and stared. One night when I was coming out of the main-floor bathroom, I saw a flash image of a small one standing outside the door. He immediately disappeared, yet I took a swipe at him anyways and told him to bugger off. The little one would appear before me a couple more times, but I ignored him or stared back until I got tired of playing that game and went back to doing whatever I was doing at the time.

Paul Hellyer, the Canadian ex–minister of defense came out in 2005 and disclosed to the public that governments around the world have identified eighty-two different alien species that have visited and continue to visit our planet. He states that they all have their own agendas for coming here and that some intentions are good, some are bad, and some are benign. All of the different species are said to be far more advanced than us in science and spirituality. This might explain how they appear in a ghostlike form to John and me. Perhaps they are remote viewing us from light-years away or from some location right here on our planet that they use as a base of operations. We are just some of the people on Earth who are able to tune in to whatever kind of frequency that they sometimes exist on, and they quietly observe us for their own reasons.

The time came within a week or so from the last email for Tony and me to conduct an investigation of the Oakville home. As it was a tiny two-bedroom basement apartment, Tony decided that only he and I would attend. We arrived and were met by Maria, her husband Chris, and her five-year-old son Brian. They explained to the son that Tony and I were there to "inspect the house", as he was fairly curious as to who these two strange men were with all of their peculiar equipment. Three night-vision cameras were set up to cover the two bedrooms and the small living room. Tony made the kitchen our base of operations and had everything connected to the monitor for real-time viewing and recording.

Brian's room was jam-packed with toys, books, electronic games, and everything else one can imagine. I had never witnessed one singular kid with so much stuff. He was a shy little man but seemed happy enough and greeted us when we walked in. Within moments he went behind his door to an area cluttered with toys and other assorted gadgets and walked out proudly with something in his hands. Tony and I looked at each other uneasily as Brian approached us with a small inflatable "Grey" alien toy. Brian took joy in showing it to us and squeezed its hand to make it squeak. His father later told us that he hadn't touched that particular toy in months and wondered aloud why he would seek it out tonight of all nights. It was an interesting "coincidence". Brian, whose pet name was Bubu, had also taken to drawing pictures of himself and his parents as beings with large heads and large black eyes. He had also asked his mother to draw an alien "Grey" on an owl-shaped blackboard, which hung in the kitchen. She wrote "Alien Bubu" above the figure.

As Tony set up more equipment and got settled, I took Maria aside to the living room to ask her some specific and possibly unsettling questions. John had explained to me that every time he believed that the Greys visited at night, he would hear a double clicking sound. He believed that however they traveled between whatever plane of existence they were on and ours, it would make a clicking sound, and they would appear. He had even set up his recorder on his nightstand and had captured the clicks. Maria looked at me anxiously when I asked her if she heard the clicking sound at night. She confirmed that she had heard it several times and always between the hours of two and three in the morning. It was the same time that John's recorder captured it at his home. While I spoke with Maria, I could see from the corner of my eye that something small and white was moving with great speed around the apartment. I didn't let on that I was seeing something, as I didn't want to upset her more than she already was.

Soon enough, I closed myself in the little boy's room as he was put to sleep in his parents' bed for the night. John and I were both convinced from our remote viewing that his room was the hot spot in the basement apartment, and I was eager to see what I might encounter in the room. I spent the good part of an hour sitting on the floor of Brian's room, conducting EVP sessions and asking whatever was there to make the K2 spike or move something in the room. I didn't have any luck with anything in there and didn't feel any type of presence with me at all.

Tony and I eventually took the investigation to the living room and asked Maria and Chris to join us. We put our recorders on the tables and produced the spirit box. The spirit box didn't offer up much of anything as we asked the usual questions. Tony then plugged headphones into the box to see if he could hear any better as we asked our questions. From the kitchen area, Maria, Chris and I heard a disembodied female voice say something that we couldn't make out. We immediately asked Tony to unplug from his headphones and told him what had happened. That was only the second time that I had ever experienced a DVP (disembodied voice phenomenon).

As we all sat in the living room and continued to chat, John texted me and said that he was at home and remote viewing the apartment. He described the apartment to a tee, and I grinned and shook my head in amazement that he had the ability to do such things. He texted me again – *She's a good-looking woman! Petite too!* I looked at Maria but didn't tell her what I had just read. I just smiled. John's viewing seemed to be on a strange lag though. He was telling me that Tony, Chris and Maria were sitting in the kitchen at the table while I was in the kid's room all alone. I confirmed that we had been doing just that, but it was almost an hour prior. He didn't have an explanation for the "lag". He then texted me and said that he sensed that there were two spirits watching us from outside the bedroom windows. Moments after he texted me this, Chris and I heard a loud double bang come from inside Brian's room. It had sounded just like someone pounding on his window with their fist. Chris and I entered the boy's room and didn't find anything out of place. I texted John and told him that the natives were restless. He had pissed someone off.

Tony and I remained for about another hour and then collected everything and retreated for home. As we began to drive down the street, Tony thought that he heard a sharp breath behind his right ear. I made it clear to whatever it may have been that it was not welcome to follow us home.

The next day Tony received an email from Maria. She told him that she was woken by her bed shaking at around two in the morning. She was getting seriously frightened and didn't know what to do. She spoke about moving away from their apartment as well.

John and I gave up on talking about the Greys and both decided that the real problem were the spirits that were in the home. *It was time to do our thing.* John and I began to remote view the apartment to see what we could come up with. I quickly got an image of a white male, late twenties or early thirties, with a tall lanky build and dirty blond hair. He had a "white trash" look to him and gave the impression to the both of us that he was a loser type who didn't amount to much in life. I picked up on the name Gary or Glenn. John confirmed the name Gary with his spirit guide. I then picked up on the look of the female spirit that was with Gary. She was short and was as round as she was tall. White with long greasy dark hair. John confirmed that when he remote viewed the apartment, he got a glimpse of her large ass as she "fled" from John.

John and I soon learned that Maria had cleaned a house at the beginning of the summer that belonged to her landlord. It was another small rental not far from where she lived now. There had been an apparent suicide in the home, and the place needed to be cleaned and made presentable for the next possible renter. Maria provided us with a Google Map image of the home for us to work from. I remote viewed the property and took my "mental" tour of the place. I found myself in the small basement apartment of the home. It was dark and unkempt, and I received flash images of painkillers. This was what I believed that Gary had used to end his life either by accident or on purpose. John and I came to the strong conclusion that Gary had taken a shine to Maria and attached himself to her. She was the kind of woman he would never have had in life, so he took it upon himself to follow her home and set up shop. The origin of the female spirit was still a mystery, as was her name. We both also got the strong impression that both Gary and the female were newly deceased.

The review of the EVPs from our investigation was a large task. It seemed that Gary and his female friend talked up a storm, and our digital recorders picked up a ton of it. When we were at the apartment, Maria offered Tony and me cold drinks. When she opened up the fridge, a female EVP said: "Grab a beer!"

Twice on the recorders a male voice came through very frustrated and angry and cried: "FUCK!"

Other EVPs that I captured:

- "Who is this...?"
- "She got fired" – This was right after Chris explained to us that Maria had got fired from her job back in Portugal when she became pregnant with Brian.
- "I can see myself there...right there..."
- "Who the hell is that?"

One piece of incredible evidence that almost floored me was when John sent me an EVP that he had recorded while remote viewing Maria's apartment and came across the Gary spirit. John told me that Gary "freaked out" on him when he arrived astrally and unleashed a tirade of verbal hostility on him. John did his best to "push" Gary out of the apartment and fill the rooms with white light as he did. When John "returned" to his home, he reviewed his recorder. There, loud and clear, was the voice of the spirit Gary saying, *"Stop it! Don't do that!"* This was all the proof that I would ever want to know that John was a hundred percent legitimate with his astounding gifts. It was incredible.

John later told me that he "visited" the Oakville apartment once again to search for signs of the Gary spirit and his female spirit friend. He told me that once he entered the apartment astrally, a large beam of light emanated from his forehead and filled the rooms with white light. It wasn't something that he made a conscious effort to do, it just happened. I joked and said that he was like Cyclops from the X-Men shooting lasers from his eyes. I then dubbed him Beacon Boy! So far, at the time of this writing, the astral cleansing worked, and Maria said that the apartment was quiet.

11

BIG JOHN

Even though I have already written quite a bit about Big John's presence and malicious actions, there is still a bit more to be said about him. He was the absolute catalyst towards John's psychic journey and the reason why John and I became connected in the first place.

Big John, whose actual name I figured out was Richard, was once a resident of the rental home that John owned. This was where John was first attacked while conducting renovations and began to quickly doubt his own skepticism and discover that spirits were an actual thing and that some could be dangerous to the living.

After my first visit to John's home, seeing the Big John apparition for myself as well as the water-mark footprints on John's beautiful hardwood floors, I felt I might be on his radar. As a big man myself – *six feet seven and 300 and none of your business pounds* – I knew it would be just a matter of time before Big John might try some of his nonsense on me. Physically I would be a challenge to a living Big John, but since he was a spirit, any torment he might send my way would have to be inflicted psychically and mentally.

When I left John's home, I had told him out loud (so Big John could hear as well) that I hoped that I wouldn't be followed home by any spirits and that Big John specifically could piss right off and stay right where he was. It wasn't long before he came to visit.

About two days after my trip to John's place, I was sitting in my family room, watching television. From inside the doorway I could see the large silhouette of a spirit watching me. It was Big John. I looked at him briefly, asked him what he wanted and, after not receiving a reply, told him to fuck right off out of my house. He did. The next morning after I woke, I looked to the wall beside my nightstand and could see the water-mark impression of a large hand. I quickly rubbed it off before my wife could see it. This was an obvious attempt at intimidation, but it didn't work. If your footprints didn't faze me, why would a handprint?

In December of 2017, Tony from SHIP and I decided to visit John and spend a full day and a sleepover with the intentions of conducting a lengthy investigation into the spirits that filled John's home. John told us that it was one of the quietest days he could remember. It was almost like they knew we were coming and collectively decided to mess with us by not communicating at all. They refused to touch the K2 meter, and as I recall, there weren't many decent EVPs from our visit. We mostly drank beer and ate chips all day.

Eventually we decided to call it a night and stumbled to our respective bedrooms for the evening. John gave me a small base-ment bedroom. A windowless room, with not much more than a bed and a small dresser, would be mine for the evening. I unpacked my CPAP machine (which keeps me from snoring like a chainsaw), hooked myself up, and hit the sack.

Just before I got in the bed and under the covers, I decided to leave my jeans on. I had visions of me having to jump up in the middle of the night and didn't want to do it in my underwear. As I rolled over on my side, a small marble-sized selenite rock that was inside my jeans pocket jammed me in the hip. A lady had given it to me and said that it would ward off psychic attacks from spirits. I took it from my pocket and placed it on the floor beside my CPAP machine. Not two minutes later something picked the rock up and slammed it up and down twice with some force on the floor. It was Big John. It had to be. I didn't react to the rock being slammed down. I closed my eyes, rolled over, and said to the room, "It's time for sleep, dude. Get lost." In the family room, right outside the bedroom door, John had several dozen slats of wood for cutting boards that he makes as a hobby. Ten minutes after the rock incident, I could distinctly hear slats of wood being thrown around the room. I resisted the urge to jump up and investigate but stood my ground (or bed) and ignored it.

In spite of the poltergeist activity, I actually fell asleep pretty quickly – copious amounts of beer can do that sometimes. I had set my alarm on my phone for eight the next morning. I awoke on my own and lit my phone up in the pitch-black room to reveal it was seven on the nose. I had one more hour of shut-eye. I rolled over on my left-hand side and had my right hand exposed above the covers and slightly elevated. Suddenly an invisible force slapped my hand quite hard. To my surprise, I remained perfectly calm and didn't react at all.

"I'm trying to get one more hour of sleep, dude. Piss off!" An hour later, I got up and flipped on the light switch. Something (take a wild guess as to who) had taken the cords of my CPAP machine and had bunched them up into a ball and laid the machine on top of them. The machine was slightly tilted now, and some of the water in its reservoir had leaked out. Asshole, I thought. I climbed the stairs to the main room and found John in his kitchen.

"How was your night?" I asked.

"Great," he replied. "I had one of the best sleeps I've had in a long time."

I then told John and Tony what had happened to me.

"That sounds like Big John," John replied. "That's totally something he would do!"

We had a quick coffee and joked about me being "tormented" throughout the night before Tony and I said our good-byes and made the two-hour drive home.

Later on that same week, John texted me a photo that his daughter had taken in her dorm room at university. There, in the photo, was a very large handprint stained on her wall. It was huge, and the fingers looked elongated and pointed at the end. John was certain that this was the work of Big John. John was upset that Big John had dropped his attention from him, and now it looked like he was making his presence known to his daughter. As John and I texted back and forth about the situation, John said that he had received a message from one of his guides that he was to remote view and look for his daughter's deceased grandfathers. This, his guide had said, is where you will find Big John.

As John remote viewed his daughter's dorm room – *he found them*. There in the corner was his own deceased father and his former father-in-law in spirit form. The two grandfathers were protecting their granddaughter from Big John and making their presence known to him. John was to point out that there was another spirit there as well, my uncle Earl. As John remote viewed the dorm room and could see the two grandfathers and my uncle, he also found Big John there as well. He texted me afterwards and gave me some amazing news. John had a strong image of my uncle Earl taking a hold of Big John's arm and guiding him towards the light. The two grandfathers were close behind and were acting as backup. He said that my uncle was being very respectful towards Big John and was patting him on the back with his other arm. Moments later they were all gone as the light consumed them. Big John was gone. Finally. Hopefully.

12

THE FERGUS GRAND THEATER

The theater in Fergus is a beautiful old limestone building that backs onto the Grand River and is a place that hosts dozens of plays and musical guests every year. Built in 1928, the theater was once the location of a barn with livestock and horses. I'm not sure where or when I first heard stories of it being haunted, but knew that it was a spot that I wanted to investigate just on its looks alone. I was surprised when the manager of the building so quickly agreed to let SHIP and me in there.

Often you will end up speaking with a skeptic or someone who is fearful of the paranormal, and the conversation ends quite quickly. This was definitely the other way around. I was given a tour of the building and a key for access. The rest of the team was excited that I had gained access to such an historic building so easily.

As I often do when checking out a new location, I took some photos with my phone and sent them to John. The basement of the theater is a damp and dark lime and fieldstone tomb with most of the floor being dirt. Naked and exposed bulbs hang from the low ceiling and give off an eerie glow. John told me that a man came through one of the far limestone walls and presented himself to him. The man was wearing very old-style clothing, possibly from the turn of the century, and was enraged that John was able to remote view him. John told me that he got the strong impression the man had once lived and worked somewhere along the same street many decades ago. I "piggy-backed" off John's energy and was able to get a clear picture of "Henry". Henry was the name that instantly came to me. John had a strong impression that I was right, and we continued with the name. Henry kept going in and out of the far wall and continued to rage at John. John told me that he was getting images of Henry stealing items off the dead and believed that he had operated an incinerator for the purposes of cremation.

About a week later, I discovered that one of the stores along the same side of the street had a very old and defunct inciner-ator in the bowels of its basement. A local historian told me that they used to use it to cremate dead livestock, as it was easier than burying them along the banks of the river. I was also told that some poor Irish may have ended up in the incinerator, as they wouldn't have had the funds, nor the family, to give them a proper burial. This was where Henry may have stolen items from the dead.

The actual night of the investigation consisted of Tony, Michelle, Danny, Barb, Corrine and an indie film-making friend of mine, Rob. Rob and I had plans at the time to film some of the investigations and to possibly make a mini documentary about them. We set up our night-vision cameras, placed recorders in random locations, and split up in various parts of the theater to begin.

Corrine and I headed for the basement and made ourselves comfortable on some very dusty and dirty cinder blocks that separated the dirt part of the floor from the concrete part. We had a recorder and K2 meter and sat in almost complete darkness. One of the night-vision cameras was set up facing us, and Tony could watch us on the main monitor from the comfort of the lobby. As we sat in the dark, Corrine kept glancing repeatedly over her right shoulder. She kept getting a strong feeling that something was back there and watching us. Tony picked up on this as he watched on the monitor. He called us on the walkie-talkie.

"Corrine, are you feeling anxious about that spot back there? You keep looking back there!" Corrine confirmed that she felt uneasy about the area and moved to a different spot on the cinder blocks so she was now facing the same direction. Tony told us that when he had been down in the same location earlier, he kept getting drawn to the same spot that Corrine was looking at and felt uneasy about it as well.

After a while, Corrine and I decided to investigate another spot inside the theater. We made our way through the dark and walked down the aisle of the main auditorium. We stumbled our way to the back of the stage and sat on some stools that we found. We had our recorder and K2 sitting on a shelf beside us. Danny was sitting in one of the back rows, facing the stage. We couldn't see him, as it was pitch black in the theater, but could see the lights on his own recorder and K2 meter. As he sat quietly in the dark, Danny told us that he could see what looked to be the outlines of heads sitting in the seats in front of him. He said it looked to be about a dozen people ahead of him quietly seated in the rows as if they were watching a performance. Moments later Corrine and I heard what sounded like the shuffling of several pairs of feet move from the area where Danny was to the right-side theater seats. The sounds of people sitting and settling in chairs could then be heard.

"Danny, is that you?" I asked.

Danny, still seated where he was originally, told me that he was hearing the same thing, and it sounded like people taking their seats somewhere along the west wall of the theater. We listened carefully as it continued for a few more moments before becoming quiet again.

John messaged me sometime during the night and told me that there was an alpha spirit there that was keeping the other spirits from communicating with us. The spirit wanted us out of the building and figured that if we didn't get any confirmation through any EVPs or any video evidence, then we would get tired of the place and leave. It was a controlling energy and had some kind of dominance over the other spirits that were in the building. It was confirmed by the other members of SHIP that it was an unusually quiet investigation and was a little disappointing to say the least. John had messaged Tony the same thoughts on the dominant spirit. As we started to pack up and get ready to leave, Tony walked into the main theater and addressed the spirits that were there.

"So, I hear that there is one of you that is keeping the others from communicating with us. Pretty sad that all of you are letting him control you and keeping you from speaking to us. You had your chance. Too bad you let him ruin it!"

John would have the alpha spirit present himself to him several times over the next few nights. John told me that he came dressed in a black robe and tried to be as intimidating and scary as possible. John brushed him off and one night even flipped him the bird and told him to fuck off. The spirit never showed up again.

13

WELLINGTON COUNTY MUSEUM

The Wellington County Museum and Archives is a National Historic Site and is located in a building that stands as the oldest remaining House of Industry in Canada. It was built in 1877 as a "poorhouse" or place of refuge for the poor, homeless, and destitute people in Wellington County. Over 600 people perished inside the facility over the years, and its walls have many dark and sordid stories to tell. There is a cemetery a few hundred yards away from the main building that contains about half of the reported deceased. Historians can only speculate as to where the other bodies ended up. Rumors of former staff abusing the elderly and mentally challenged fill the archives. A place of refuge became a place of mistreatment and abuse for many. From the outside, it is a big bold and archaic building, which casts an ominous shadow from its elevated position. The current staff say that there isn't a day that goes by when some random traveler doesn't pop in to ask if it is haunted. It certainly looks like it is.

Due to the building's history and its ominous appearance, it has become a location of envy for paranormal investigators from all over the province. It was a veritable brass ring for ghost hunters. For years and years teams have tried to gain access to the building and grounds to be the first ones in. A stoic staff member of the museum voiced concerns that the history of the building was to be preserved and that the past residents don't become overlooked or forgotten by ghost stories. The SHIP team had expressed their own desires to gain access to the building but knew that it wasn't going to happen for them. I saw this as a challenge and joked that I would get the team access to the building, and we would be the first paranormal team to be allowed to investigate.

I made the long, arduous three-minute drive to the building from my home (I literally could have walked) and presented myself to the receptionist. I was ready for an argument and had made mental preparations to make a valid argument for me and SHIP being allowed in. It took me all of about two minutes to get permission. The museum staff told me that they finally wanted to make use of the building's haunted notoriety, cash in on that mystique, and would be happy to have us. Well, shoot, that was easy. My timing had been perfect, and I wondered if there were some outside forces gently nudging me along. I then arranged with Kyle, one of the museum's staff members, for him to join us on the evening of the ghost hunt. He would grant us access to the building and be our chaperon for the duration of the investigation. Kyle claimed that he was a skeptic and didn't have any of his own ghost stories to tell from working in the building. I quietly hoped to change all that.

The night of the investigation came quickly, and we were all excited to be granted access to the location. When I had told the team that I had received permission, there were wide eyes, gaping mouths, and then a slew of high fives and smiles all around. It was a small proud little victory for all of us. The team would consist of Tony, myself, Barb, Michelle, a former team member (who shall remain nameless), and Danny B. We would all try to pair up and head off to different sections of the huge building. Tony decided to set up a base of operations in the main hallway of the second level. This would consist of a folding table with the camera monitors on it, and a handheld radio for contacting members of the team. The upper level of the museum had several rooms with different themes to them that were all connected by one main hallway. Below us was the former main entrance to the building with an art gallery, and a couple of other rooms that had random exhibits in them.

One room on the second floor had a replica World War I trench in it, complete with piped-in sounds of battle. Mannequins wore vintage-era Canadian army uniforms and added their own brand of creepiness to the area. Their eyes seemed to follow you as you moved around the room, and in the dim lighting we all half expected one of them to jump up. The other rooms consisted of historic themes, varying from an indigenous setting with wildlife, to another room with a replica kitchen setting from the turn of the century. Another room at the opposite end of the hall from the war room was dubbed "the log cabin". This room had a reputation among visitors of giving off an uncomfortable vibe, and several people reported to staff that they felt like they had been touched or were overcome with a desire to quickly leave.

The museum also has a massive attic, which stores antique archived furniture, old televisions with the round screens, radios, spinning wheels and even a very old child-size casket in one corner. Michelle and I spent some time in there with Kyle in tow but didn't pick up on anything. Back in the log cabin room, Tony and the nameless former team member attempted to conduct some EVP sessions and use the spirit box. They both came downstairs to the main level, where Kyle, Michelle and I were taking a break in a conference-style room. Tony said that they both came under psychic attack and that they were both overwhelmed with a strong headache and signs of dizziness. They felt it best to leave the room and get some fresh air. Whatever was in the room with them wanted them gone and had succeeded. Later on, Tony and I entered the log cabin room while Michelle took her turn at our command post. Kyle sat on the floor behind her and could hear us fire up the spirit box. Tony and I asked questions to the possible spirits in the room.

One question I asked was met with a remarkably clear answer through the spirit box. *"Who is this?"* came the male voice in response to my question.

"This is Dan," I said. "Who are you?" No more responses came.

We all remarked on how clear the voice was. Even Kyle the skeptic took notice of the strong male voice, and I wondered quietly if we were slowly making him a believer. Later on during another break in the conference room (which used to be the male hospital ward) we all saw a dark shadow move along the far wall and head for a doorway. Kyle, who was sitting across from me at the table, even turned his head and watched this quick apparition.

"What did you see there, Kyle?" I asked with a smile on my face. Kyle gave off a funny look, and I could see him struggling for an answer. "That's a ghost, Kyle!" I said, leaning in for dramatic effect. I don't think he gave me a good enough skeptical *or* logical reason for the shadow phenomenon, and we left it at that.

There are a series of service hallways that staff refer to as *"the Tunnels."* They run along the main floor and aren't even subterranean. The tunnels lead to electrical rooms, different parts of the building, and the old defunct furnace room, which used to heat the building many years ago. The old furnace area looks like Freddy Kruger's living room and in the dark, with only the glow of the exit signs, is pretty creepy. The old coal furnaces are still there and radiate an ominous energy, which fills the room. A perfect place to film a horror movie for sure. I went down there alone and sat in the dark. I had a heavy feeling come over me while down there, but after many requests to the spirits, they wanted nothing to do with me. I often wonder when people die, if they are often mentally stuck in the era that they lived in. A digital recorder, cell phone, and the other strange gizmos we use for ghost hunting might be intimidating to them. They might be confused as to their purpose and might think that it might be something that could actually harm them. I always make a point of explaining to them what the gadget in my hand is and what it's used for.

On the same property of the museum is a large old wooden barn. It is used as part of the museum and has an upper and lower level. The main floor contains displays holding old farming tools, various grains that would have been planted on the grounds, and basically anything else a barn would hold. It also has several archived photos of the residents who worked and lived there. The lower level was where livestock would have been kept, and there are two very large replica horses that, like the mannequins in the main building, had eyes that seemed to follow you. There were a few EVPs captured in the barn, and Tony caught on film a very large shadow man standing in one of the doorways. Throughout the night, I could sense that there were tons of spirits watching us from a distance, but they were holding back and quietly observing. Our team was a strange phenomenon for them and made them keep their distance for sure.

As part of our admittance into the museum as a paranormal team, Kyle and the rest of the management wanted us to host an evening where we would present our ghostly findings to an audience. We readily agreed and picked our best EVPs and photos from the evening. Tony went above and beyond and created a fantastic PowerPoint presentation. Our event sold out quickly, and just over a hundred people from the area bought tickets to attend. It had sold out fast, and townsfolk were still asking for tickets on the day of the event.

It went to show how popular the lore and the mystery of the building was. Tony warmed up the crowd with some of his best EVPs from other investigations and even showed the short video of the cupboard opening by itself from the Clifford home. One of the more frightening EVPs we played for the crowd was a type of very loud hissing/growl that was captured on one of our recorders while we were setting up our equipment and planning out the night. Something was not happy that we were there and was attempting to make itself known. It was the first time I had ever heard anything *"demonic"* come through our recorders, and it was exciting as well.

Everyone loved the presentation, and by a show of hands, only one person raised their arm when I asked if there were any nonbelievers in the room. The lady was quick to admit though that we had probably changed her mind. Kyle to this day (although I think reluctantly) remains a skeptic.

Afterwards, John and I were able to zero in on the spirit that haunted the log cabin room. He was a large-framed man wearing blue denim coveralls and a collared shirt. He seemed to be suffering from some type of mental illness and was angry with all the visitors coming into his area. He felt like the log cabin room was his domain, and he stored and exerted his energy to make people feel uncomfortable and want to leave the area as quickly as possible. We didn't bother to try to move him, as we felt that he wouldn't want to leave anyways. He was a part of the museum for as long as he wished.

14

SOME OF THE EVP'S COLLECTED FROM
THE POORHOUSE INVESTIGATION

The transcripts of these EVPs are directly taken from Tony's notes. **No edits.**
Elora Poor House
Sept 30 2017

Investigators: Barb, Michelle, Dan B, Dan H, Tony along with care taker Kyle.

0.21 - **Bull shit** *(male)* - Kyle talking about many people buried on the site. Spirits know more?

1.24 - **Barbara** *(male)*. Barb is talking.

3.09 - group is doing a tour of the place – basement first.

12.30 - electrical interference in the tunnels.

16.08 - electrical interference stops.

16.37 - **going on** - *(male)* - Tony mentions that the hair on his arm is standing up.

18.16 - overhearing Dan & Dan B having some contact in the tunnel.

18.59 - **overcoat** *(male)* -

19.26 - **your phone** *(male-deep voice)* - Tony telling group to turn off their phones. Electrical static.

19.44 - **yes** *(male)* -

25.39 - **yell?** *(male)* - group upstairs in old hospital room and Kyle talking about the place once was a senior's home.

34.03 - **think they're frighten?** *(male whispering)* - Tony & Barb went up the wrong stairway.

37.59 - **Liar** *(male)* - Spirit disagreeing what Kyle was saying about the separation of female and males sleeping quarters.

39.59 - **male yelling** – Group moved towards the war room but recorder was still in log room.

48.25 - **you burke off?** *(male)* laying out the cable into the log room. (not exactly sure what's being said there).

55.40 - **the guy is L S D?** - ***** just left the log room setting up the cameras.

59.17 - **I was going to kill him** *(male)* - Tony, ***** and Barb setting up cameras in log room.

208.11 - **let me out** *(male)* - group just arrives back to the third floor after 20 minutes of silence.

208.16 - **I'll freeze them?** - Just Dan & Tony at the table in the third-floor hall way.

208.30 - **Who's that for** – Tony id replacing batteries in the walkie talkie.

227.00 - Tony experience a sharp pain in his back.

229.47 - **I'm going to hit you punk** *(male)* - Just after my back pain.

236.51 - ***** & Tony get a whiff of wood burning smoke at the same time.

237.02 - **clear the building** *(male)*.

237.25 - time check – 21.05.

300.25 – **move your car, Ruth?** *(male)* - group working on a piece of gear.

301.29 - your not very interesting. *(Male)* – Group working on equipment.

307.20 - Tony & Michael in War Room – Ghost box turn on.

308.20 - sit *(male)* - GB.

308.28 - do I like girls *(male)* - GB- Tony asked who was there?

308.40 - pssst not *(male)* - Michael heard partial GB and asked if the spirit think we look like girls?

308.44 - sure *(male)* GB – Tony asked if the spirits can give us a name?

308.49 - modge *(male)* - Tony asked for a name?

309.38 - modge? *(male)* GB (VF) - Tony asked for the name again.

311.10 - female voice? (#26).

311.15 - we just dead? *(male)*.

312.18 - voices??

315.12 - I would agree *(male)* GB – Tony asked if the Ross rifle was good?

316.24 - Tony enters another room.

318.21 - Tony turns on the GB.

318.52 - you think this was familiar. *(male)* - Heard after Tony talking. Dan's camera batteries died. (in logged room). Heard by group but couldn't pick out.

319.13 - bottom. *(male)* - Heard by Tony.

319.53 - fire me or firemen *(male)* (VF) – Tony asked who the spirit was?

320.13 - don't tell or **Hotel?** - *(male)* Tony asked for a name again.

320.40 - stupid *(male)* (VF) - Michael asked the spirit what his name was.

32.25 - no trade *(male)* GB - Tony asked the spirits what trade they were?

15

ALICE

As you will see, John plays a very big part of most of my paranormal experiences. A prominent psychic medium told me that he and I had a very strong connection and may have been connected in a previous life. I'm not a big believer in reincarnation, but I accepted her statement and let that be an explanation for now. This connection, however, became one of our strengths when dealing with malicious spirits.

John got "volunteered" by his significant other to help her with a house-painting job that she had been hired for. Being the good person that he is, he reluctantly agreed and accompanied her to the home. As John climbed a ladder on the southeast side of the house, he stopped at a large window to begin painting. From the window, the spirit of an older lady suddenly appeared in view and startled him so bad that he almost fell off the ladder. John steadied himself and heard a female voice inside his head say, *"See what I can do...?"* Minutes later as John calmed himself down and tried to regain his composure on the ladder, the neighbors, a man and his sister, began arguing and shouting at each other in the backyard. Moments later, the man's wife came out and began arguing along with them. Once again John heard the female voice, *"See what I can do...?"*

John continued on with painting his side of the house and ignored this nasty old female spirit. As he layered paint on to the home, he casually looked over to the other house beside the property and could see a large selenite lamp in the window of a bedroom. Obviously this old woman spirit was a nuisance to others, and one of the neighbors had taken some measure in protecting their home from her. John was tempted to knock on the door and ask about the lamp but knew that his fiancé would kill him if he did.

Eventually they finished for the day and went home. John messaged me as to what had happened to him at the home. As John messaged me, the female spirit appeared in his living room and started to rant and rave at him. She was clearly pissed that John was talking about her to me. I instantly connected with this woman and knew immediately that her name was Alice. She was wearing a white knit cardigan, bluish-gray slacks and had tight white curly hair. Her anger and anxiety was radiating from her, and I could feel it. She was super pissed off! I remotely approached Alice and bathed her in white light. At the same time, I could see my hands on her shoulders and asked her to calm down. Her anger and anxiety were overwhelming. I could feel it physically as I sat in my bedroom a two-hour drive away from John's home. I continued to ask her to calm down. I told her that she needed to move on and that she would be fine if she did. Just then a strong message came to me, and I messaged John. "Tell her that Robert is waiting for her, and she needs to go with him." John confirmed that an older gentleman had just appeared in his kitchen doorway and was waiting for Alice. I continued to try to soothe her. An image of her in a tiny apartment came to me. In the image, which kept repeating itself to me, I could see Alice cross in front of a couch in a living room and then collapse to the floor. A sudden heart attack had taken her life. I continued to calm Alice down and asked her to go with Robert. I was then disconnected from John's living room, and an image of an old black-and-white photo of Alice and her husband Robert came to me. Both of them were much younger, smiling and happy in the photo. I believe it was perhaps Robert's way of projecting to me that John and I had done our jobs and helped her move on.

We concluded that Alice had been a lonely childless widow for quite some time, and her misery had overtaken her emotionally in life and in death. John and I felt good about what we had accomplished that night. That was the very first time we had moved a spirit on.

16

HAMILTON POLTERGEIST

Tony contacted me and let me know that we might have another investigation coming up soon. A despondent young mother had reached out to him through his online ad and said that they were having some very strange occurrences in their new home. The mother, whom I will call Lisa, said that they had just moved in to a new rental property in Hamilton and were having unexplained things going on. Chairs would rock on their own, shadow figures could be seen moving about, a certain door to the basement would open on its own, and other oddities occurred that they couldn't explain. Lisa was even able to capture on her cell phone a towel moving on its own as it hung on the end of a couch.

A short time before all this, John had placed an ad on the same website as Tony and offered his services to aid anyone having issues with unwanted spiritual activity. Lisa, not knowing that Tony and SHIP were connected to John in any way, reached out to him at the same time. A nice coincidence. John began to remote view the property to locate the source of the paranormal activity.

A little later, John texted me and said that once he began to remote view the home, a tall figure wearing a gray hooded robe covered in ancient "demonic" symbols appeared at his place. John, now being used to such things, and not the poor nervous wreck he used to be when Big John had come into the picture, took the "demon's" presence in stride. John was becoming increasingly confident towards such manifestations and looked forward to any challenges that might come his way. I was eager as well. This demon presented himself to John in hopes of scaring him off but failed miserably. John continued to remote view the entity but was unable to get a good read off of it. He only stated that he believed that it was a low-level poltergeist. John ignored the entity and continued to remote view the home. John would astrally project himself throughout the house and blast white light into every nook and cranny in hopes of protecting the family – especially the children. The kids in the home had been affected by the poltergeist and took to moving their mattresses from their beds to the floor of their parents' bedroom for safety and comfort.

Often when John and I would communicate and discuss what was going on at a certain property, whatever (or whomever) he was trying to deal with would suddenly appear at my home. Our antennas would be up, and the spirits would zero in on either John or myself. This time I wouldn't have a visitor to my place. I was a little disappointed.

A couple of days later, Tony and I made the daytime trek to Hamilton to see the family and discuss what we could do for them. John told me that he believed that the home was very close to an industrial complex and that the home had green shingles. When Tony and I arrived at the home, it was indeed literally across the road from an industrial complex, and there were some green shingles peeking out from under some newer gray-colored ones. John was bang on once again. The home, being a rental in a very blue-collar area of Hamilton, was a little rough looking. It was very close to the street, had a yard full of junk, and needed some serious cosmetic care. Tony and I entered and met Lisa face-to-face. She was accompanied by her husband and another gentleman, who was the father of her four children. *An odd living arrangement but who am I to judge?*

Tony sat at the dining room table with the three adults and began to ask them his usual preliminary questions. I immediately headed for the basement, as I wanted to meet the poltergeist face-to-face. The basement was a gray concrete bunker with a very low ceiling. Being so tall, I had to walk around hunched right over with my hands on my knees for support. I found a dusty old chair to sit on and took my recorder out. Almost immediately to my left I saw him. A gray hooded figure appeared not ten feet away from me. His flowing robe swept across the floor as he attempted to manifest in front of me. I took my recorder out in hopes that he would actually answer some questions. Suddenly the door to the basement burst open, and a middle-aged East Indian man came down the stairs. The entity vanished immediately. The man was the landlord and had come unannounced, stating that he was there to collect junk from the backyard to make it fairly presentable for the new tenants. *Shit.*

I squeezed my way back up the narrow rickety stairs and found Tony still at the dining room table, gabbing away with the trio. I joined him at the table and, when I had a moment, told him that our day was a bust. He agreed that there were just too many people in the home and too much activity going on around us, and even a preliminary investigation would be impossible. I entertained myself with a new puppy that the family had while Tony wrapped things up.

The next day Lisa had texted John and Tony and told them both that there was a handheld circular saw sitting on a basement shelf and that it would turn on by itself. Apparently the

poltergeist in the home was ramping up his game in his attempts
to unhinge the people who lived there. Lisa was even able to
record on video the sound of the saw coming on by itself as
everyone else watched TV in the living room. I heard the two
men in the video start to get upset and panic a little bit as Lisa
remained calm and told them not to acknowledge it. I had told
her that before I had left the home, and it was nice to hear that
she was taking my advice. Nice to see that she was a lot tougher
than the two men too.

That night John remote viewed the house once again, and
this time was able to confront the poltergeist. John texted me
and said that he had the entity cornered in the basement and
was projecting white light on him to trap him. The facade of the
gray robe with the demonic images faded, and John and I were
able to see the "demon" in his true state. I connected remotely
and saw the image of a young man, maybe twenty years old. He
had short brown hair, a pasty complexion, along with acne on
his chin, and was wearing regular clothes. The name David
came to me. John said that David was ranting like a madman.
David was a troubled person who had been raised by shitty
parents. He died young from a suicide and had either resided in
the same home at one point or had lived close by. David
resented Lisa and didn't like the way she sometimes spoke to her
children and did not approve of her having two men in her bed.
His actions and anger were more against her than anyone else in
the home. The others were just collateral damage, so to speak.
John asked me to *do my thing* as he confined David in white
light. I got a close image of David as he stood there in the basement. I projected myself and told him that he had to move on
and wasn't welcome in the home. I explained to him that he
didn't have to fear the light and that he wouldn't be judged for
the person that he used to be. I could feel his anxiety and panic
as I projected to him. I reiterated what I said several times, and

even asked my uncle Earl to provide David with some help moving along. As I projected, I suddenly saw a kind of bluish tunnel form. In my mind's eye it was on an angle rising up and to my right. Rings of energy pulsated around it, and as it formed, I saw a large blue "orb" of energy propel itself into it, followed by two more orbs. I knew then that David had accepted what John and I were trying to do for him, and he moved on. Perhaps the other two orbs were other spirits in the area waiting for the opportunity to move on, or there was some guided help for us. My uncle could have been one of them, I suppose.

We had successfully moved our second spirit. I felt good about it and hoped that there would be more.

John and I both accepted the fact that our abilities were given to us for a reason and this would be a service we could provide for people. Lisa confirmed with Tony over the next couple of days that the home was quiet. The atmosphere was lighter, and everything was as it should have been.

17

WATERLOO HOME

I n my hopes of making more connections with people who were interested in the paranormal and also to promote the podcast, I joined several Facebook groups that were devoted to spirits and anything else that went bump in the night. One such group was one based in Ontario. Its sole purpose was to assist people who were having issues with possible spirits and things they couldn't explain. One lady, whom I shall call Ava, posted on the group's page that she was having issues with strange noises, a glass sliding door moving on its own, a shadow person, and odd feelings in the atmosphere of the home. I sent her a message to ask if John and I could help. I also messaged John about making contact with Ava. Immediately John texted me back. "Ask her if her floors and walls in her kitchen are all white." Ava confirmed that her kitchen tiles were white and the walls were an off-white. John amazed me again with his skills. He also asked if she was having issues with weird noises. Bang on again! Then John messaged and told me that the basement was where she was having the most issues. I messaged Ava, and she was shocked and a little freaked that John was absolutely right. I then asked her to take some photos of her basement and send them to me. Her walls and carpet were all an off-white color. John was forwarded the pics, and he began to remote view the home.

One of the things that John and I have been trying to figure out is, when he is remote viewing a home, and I am "connected" in some way, is he amplifying his signal to me, or am I making use of his personal psychic energy and I am coming in that way? Either way, I had a clear image of a young male in the home. He was wearing a short-sleeved button-up shirt, blue jeans, and had wavy strawberry blond hair. John told me that he could only see him in black and white. The name Darryl immediately came to me. As I watched Darryl, he looked down and had a vacant look on his face. He wouldn't make any eye contact with either one of us. John said he just kept repeating, *"Sorry...sorry...sorry..."* John then cornered Darryl in the laundry room of the basement and embraced him in white light. I moved in to do my thing. I told Darryl that he had to move on and that he would be fine once he passed on into the light. I told him that there was no one to judge him and there would be people to connect with him and take care of him. I told him that my uncle Earl might be there to show him the way as well. Moments later a muddled image of a dull white light emerged in my mind's eye, and Darryl was gone. I told John that I had a strong feeling that Darryl had suffered from mental health issues and possibly autism when he was living. This might explain the lack of eye contact and the repetitive apologies. John agreed with me on this, and we felt that we had successfully moved Darryl to a happier spot.

I messaged Ava and told her what we had done. I also explained that the spirit looked like he was suffering from mental health issues. Ava then told me that she worked with mentally ill "clients". People who suffered from an assortment of mental health issues and also those on the autism spectrum. Holy crap, I thought. John and I were bang on again. Days later I connected with Ava again, and she said that the house was peaceful and quiet.

18

THE MAGICAL FOREST

There is a park in Fergus that runs alongside the banks of the Grand River. A beautiful spot where people hike, picnic and fish. A park that I had never actually visited before, even after living in the area for almost fourteen years. The park was given the unofficial name *"the Magical Forest"*, as it was a great place where teens could go hide from the eyes of the public, and the police, to smoke weed and drink beer in relative privacy. For some reason I came to believe that the park was haunted and asked the SHIP team to conduct a mini investigation.

Tony, Michelle, Barb and I went down to the park one summer's eve after having a meeting at one of the local pubs. The air was hot and humid, and the mosquitoes were thirsty. I separated from the group and went down one trail to conduct some EVP sessions on my own. I spent a few minutes asking questions to the possible spirits there and then headed back to the group. We made our way down one of the trails that led to a small wooden bridge that crossed a tiny creek. Before getting there, Barb and I looked back along the path that we had just taken and were amazed at what we saw! There, walking away from the path that we were just on, and towards the direction of the street, was what we could only describe as a pair of black legs walking on their own. It literally looked like a phantom pair of black pants moving along the forest floor. The feet were barely tangible, and there wasn't any torso that we could make out. Yet the legs moved with purpose and appeared to be that of a young man. Barb and I looked at each other and were excited at what we had just witnessed. Tony and Michelle were slightly ahead of us and facing the opposite direction and completely missed what we had just witnessed.

Tony conducted some spirit box sessions, and we did receive some intelligent responses from it. Michelle believed that the area had been a stopping point for Natives for when they were passing through the area. The river would have been a good stop for water and food, and the possibility that there may have been some Indigenous peoples buried in this area was pretty high. The park was also literally steps away from the local hospital, and spirits may have wandered towards the river as a source of energy.

The park is also steps away from the rear of the local hospital. Many people have reported seeing the ghost of the late Dr. Abraham Groves (whom the hospital is named after) prowling the back parking lot. There are rumors that Dr. Groves would pay grave robbers to unearth recently deceased people from the nearby cemetery so he could perform medical techniques and experiments on the cadavers. Where he disposed of them afterwards is a mystery, but many speculate that the park would have been a perfect location. Dr. Groves was also the first physician in North America to perform an appendectomy. Perhaps the stolen corpses had a part in that groundbreaking procedure.

We wandered the trails and banks of the river for about an hour. It soon got dark, and the bugs were driving us mad. We were also getting dive-bombed by bats. I hate bats.

The team made their way back to the main clearing of the park, where there was a gazebo and picnic benches. I sat down on the bench under the gazebo and took my cell phone out to conduct some "burst EVPs". This is where you listen to your recorder right after asking questions instead of listening at home when you have the opportunity to run it through a computer audio system. I quieted down and asked some questions. I asked whomever might have been there with me if they used to live in the area; were they Native? Are you the man whom Barb and I saw? I asked a couple more questions until the final one where I got a clear response. "What town are we in?" I asked. A ghostly whisper responded, *"This...is... Fergus..."* An intelligent response to a sound question. I was excited. I called Tony and Michelle over and played it for them. They could hear it clearly and were excited about it as well.

As Tony and I talked and speculated about the spirits that might reside in the park, we could clearly hear footsteps in the grass right behind us. They sounded like they were literally a few feet away and approaching us. We turned and looked but couldn't see anything at all. We conducted another burst EVP session but didn't get any responses to anything we asked. The source of the audible footsteps remained a mystery.

Later on that week when we listened to our digital recorders that we'd had going since we arrived at the park, we had some very odd noises come through. Tony's recorder had picked up an aggressive growl. It was mere moments after he had got out of his vehicle and hadn't even left the parking lot yet. I had never considered anything might be of a "demonic" nature in the park, so it was a bit of a shock for all of us to hear it.

When I was alone and on another path from everyone else, I picked up what sounded like a "raspberry". The kind of sound a little kid would make by sticking their tongue out and blowing air. I suppose it's possible that a spirit was playing around with me. A prankster and a growler all in the same area.

The park is somewhere I would like to conduct a full and proper investigation. The problem is the possibility of running into other people at all hours of the night, and the fact that there aren't any outlets for electricity. We wouldn't be able to set up any night-vision cameras and have a base camp. It also goes to show that spirits can be anywhere and everywhere. I suppose a public park is no exception.

19

THE RETURN OF BIG JOHN

In June of 2018, John and I got word that, mere steps away from his rental home, there was a house with lots of aggressive paranormal activity. The family was having a rough time dealing with what was going on and were at their wits' end. They were torn as to what to do about reaching out for help. They didn't want people around them to know what was going on in their home for fear of being shunned or treated differently by their friends and the community. The home was also for sale, and they didn't want news of it being terribly haunted getting out.

As soon as John heard about this, he had an awful feeling. *Big John was back.* He hadn't presented himself to him, but he was getting visions of him laughing at him. I did my own projecting and tried to connect and locate Big John. I sensed him and picked up on a female spirit that was with Big John. The name "Joanne" came to me. I tried to offer John some positive thoughts and offered up the idea that it wasn't Big John at all but perhaps another spirit that resembled him or was projecting as him. John was polite and accepted the idea, but he knew deep down the tormenting asshole had returned. John messaged me the next night and confirmed his fears. Big John had presented himself to John in his living room right in front of him. He stood there taunting and laughing. John texted me...

John – He's officially back! Walked into living room.

Me – Get a pic!

John – Every time I try to take a picture it won't work Me – Messing with your phone?

John – Ya, and day I told you I thought he was back crazy power draining going on. Last two nights I've been woken up at 4:11. Supposed to mean something but I'm not sure. Maybe address of home (that Big John was in now)

John and I messaged about some other things that were going on in our paranormal lives and briefly forgot about Big John. John then sent me a picture of his living room. His cat was standing on the ottoman and looking at the doorway to the kitchen. In the pic there was a white ghostly haze, and I could see a faint outline of a giant of a man standing in the doorway.

John – Kitty no like activity

Me – BJ projecting himself as huge! Bigger than before.

John – Yep, in my kitchen, big fucker.

Me – He has woman with him. Joanne or Joanna.

John – On original EVP there was a couple women. I always believed one was his wife and she was so beat up and controlled. She didn't say shit about the stuff that he was up to.

Me – Got a wee chill from that.

John then told me that there was a female spirit in his home and that she just ran across his basement. She kept going behind him, and he described her as a small lady with light brown hair. John told me that he got an image of the other home that Big John was harassing. He said it wasn't far from his rental and described it as an old gray house with a porch. John, unbeknownst to me, was remote viewing the home. As he mentally entered the other home, he found Big John in the living room, looking right at him. He messaged me...

John – I got him! Picture an old house. Walk in off a covered porch. Stairs in as soon as you walk in. Family room to the left. He's in family room. Do your thing and be an asshole!

I wasn't quite sure what John meant by *"...be an asshole!"* but I am certain he meant not to pull any punches and come on very aggressive.

I shut the TV off, set my phone down, and lay back in my chair. I closed my eyes and started to project myself. Instantly I was on the porch of this home that John had described. I entered the main entrance through a screen door and, turning to my left, could see the room that John messaged me about. There in the back corner from me was a very shocked-looking Big John. He wasn't projecting himself as a huge man anymore. He was more like six feet tall with a moderate frame. A fireplace was on the other wall to his right. He looked bewildered as to what was happening and perplexed that John and I were standing in front of him in our astral forms. He looked very anxious and frantic as if he was going to run from the area but was trapped and had nowhere to go. I charged into him and drove him back against the wall.

A flurry of kicks and punches came from my astral form as I began to lay the mother of all beatings on Big John. He tried to cover himself up, but I pushed his arms out and away from his face and threw him to the floor. I began soccer kicking him in the stomach and ribs, never giving him a second to gain any sense of composure. In my mind I screamed at him to leave everyone the fuck alone and to leave this house. I called him every name in the book as I continued to pound him. I then

suddenly found myself backing off and watched as the spirits of
my uncle Earl and Uncle Bud suddenly appeared. They rang a
few shots of their own down on Big John and then dragged him
by the neck out the front door. They literally scooped him up by
the neck and shoulders and hauled him away. I saw an astral
image of the three of them being swept up towards the sky. To
my left the spirit of a woman with short curly brown hair tried
to rush past me. I whipped around and grabbed her by the
lapels. This was the woman whom I believed to be Joanne. She
had a frightened look on her face, and her mouth gaped open
like she wanted to say something. I yelled at her to get the fuck
out of the house and to stop being a bitch. I then pivoted sharply
and threw her towards the door, where she quickly disappeared.

In the doorway to the room was John himself. He looked
pissed and winded like he had just been in a fight. He was
wearing a black T-shirt and blue jeans and made eye contact
with me. I opened my eyes, stunned as to what had just
happened. *I have one hell of an imagination,* I thought. There was
absolutely no way what had just happened was real. I texted
John and tried to be casual about it...

    Me – Anything happen?
        John – Who was kicking him? You or your uncle?
        Me – Holy F John!! That was me. I was going nuts on
    the guy.
        John – Ya, I watched it!
        Me – I had him down on the floor and I was using him as a
    soccer ball!!! I got an image of my uncles laying some beats too.
        John – Yep. I saw tons of kicks and then punches to the
    head. I kicked him in the sack for the heck of it.

We messaged our excitement to each other for a few more
minutes. John confirmed that he was wearing a black T-shirt

and blue jeans and there had been a fireplace in the room against the far wall. He could also see my uncles in there assisting us. This was wild!

John said that when he first remote viewed the home and saw Big John, the spirit had got right up in his face and threatened to kill him. That was when John actually had thrown some of his own punches and elbows before I arrived. I could feel myself being a little wound up afterwards and had some adrenaline flowing. I couldn't believe what was happening with me, and the fact that I had just astral projected myself to a home almost two hours away to kick the shit out of a dead guy! This was something that I needed more answers to but didn't know where to look. Everything had been in full color as well. That was a first for me, as previous images always seemed to be black and white. I wondered why this one had been different than the others. The ease with which I had homed in on the actual house that John only gave me a description of was shocking to me as well. To this day, John and I talk about that incident and shake our heads at the memory of it.

The next day John messaged me...

John – Got to give him credit. The big guy is here! What?! I couldn't believe it.

We had laid the mother of all ass kickings on Big John, and he had the audacity and nerve to show up again at John's house the very next evening. John told me that Big John was ape-shit mad, but John was just ignoring him. I joked and asked John if he wanted me to astrally drop the fridge on Big John's head. We talked via text some more and pondered the reason for Big John's death, why he was such a douchebag, and what we could do to get rid of him permanently. He was a special spiritual case, that was for certain. I wondered if we would tangle with him again.

Months later, John was having some issues with some shadow people running around his home, and he was getting tired of it. He messaged me and thought that Big John had come back and had brought some friends with him. John waited a few more moments and then messaged me again. "He's in my basement," he messaged. "Let's do our thing."

The sheer audacity that this spirit had was incredible. Here he was back in John's home and trying to cause shit once again. We had his number in the way of the ass kicking we had administered, but I guess you can't fix stupid. I closed my eyes and projected myself to John's home and found myself in the basement alone. I couldn't see Big John, or John himself for that matter, and wondered why it was harder this time. I remained in the center of the room and tried to focus. To my left, a young man in his mid-twenties, with short brown curly hair, brown pants, and a brown and white plaid shirt appeared. He saw me notice him, and he tried to take off. Instantly I was upon him and grabbed him by the suspenders. I whipped him around and saw his astral form get ejected out of the room and out on to the back lawn. He made an attempt to come back in but was unable to for some reason. I looked about the room in search of the main protagonist but couldn't find anyone. I opened my eyes up back home and messaged John to tell him what had happened.

John told me that he had confronted Big John in the basement and that, "One of your uncles was there to help." John didn't specify which uncle it was, but I believed it to be Earl. John and my uncle drove Big John out of the house but hadn't noticed my interaction with Big John's sidekick. As of this writing, that was (so far) the last time we had come "face-to-face" with the big jerk.

20

THE PHANTOM FACTION

John is the kind of person/psychic/medium/weirdo who gets messages in the form of very lucid and vivid dreams. In the fall of 2017 he had a dream that he was to become part of a podcast, and its goal was to help people having issues with the paranormal. As most of us do, John forgot about the dream and never thought much of it after that. At the end of the Fergus theater investigation, I had my own ideas come to me for a podcast. Danny, one of the SHIP members, is a professional radio announcer (I won't say where), has a great voice, a real gift for interviewing people, and obviously – a love of all things paranormal. I asked him what he thought about doing a podcast with John and me.

He said that he really liked the idea and was definitely interested. Neither he nor I knew about John's dream.

The next day I messaged John and told him about the idea for the podcast. John had just had his second dream in regard to this in the past few days. He told me that in his dreams he is often able to interact with whomever is sending the message. He told them that he liked the idea of it but had zero clues as how to start one, get it out to the public, and didn't have the technical know-how to do such a thing. The response to him was that, *"It's all been taken care of."* Obviously a spirit was behind it and had planted the seeds in Danny and me as well. We weren't quite sure as to why we were all being "guided" to start the podcast, but we didn't dwell on it either. We came to accept all of the *"synchronizations"* in our lives and kept moving forward.

Over the next little while I took off with the idea. I came up with some different names for the podcast, a logo, and spoke to some other people who had their own podcasts and asked for advice. One of the names I proposed was the Phantom Faction. Danny liked it right off, but John was hesitant. After a day or two he finally came to like it and accepted the name. He liked the word "faction", as it means a group, and that's what we were. We would use the podcast to reach out to others and ask them to become part of our "faction". It was official, we were now the Phantom Faction Podcast. I designed a cute but likeable Grim Reaper mascot, created a Facebook page, and had business cards made. Now it was time to record.

Danny received permission to record in a local radio station after hours. It was all sound booths, state-of-the-art recording equipment, and since we were the only ones in there, all the privacy we needed. Yet John and I were to quickly find out that we were to have many visitors inside the station. The first night we were to record, John and I entered the building with Danny from a back entrance. Once we stepped inside, John and I could feel the undeniable presence of spiritual energy. It was just like the sensation that I had back in my studio office when I walked through the door. The energy was thick and crawled up my back and right arm. Danny didn't sense anything and just smiled as John and I got shivers up our backs. Once inside the actual studio, we sat down to talk about our plan for the first recording. We believed that the first pod would be more of an introduction of ourselves to our listeners and give a little history as to how we came to be involved in the paranormal. As we sat there, John and I could see spirits moving around us. There was also a dark spirit of a man standing in the hallway, watching us. We believed that there were spirits there that were curious as to what we were up to and also believed that there were some that wanted us to fail and wished us ill fortune.

As we were leaving after that first recording, we paused in the area where we had felt all the energy. John and I could see a man walk across the room in front of us. We then described him to Danny. He smiled and was certain that it was a gentleman whom he had worked with for many years. John said that he picked up that the man really loved his job and that the radio station was his home away from home. Danny confirmed it all. John looked around the room and was grinning from ear to ear. When I asked him what he was smiling about, he said that it was nice to be surrounded by positive spirits for a change and not the assholes that he usually dealt with.

The first podcast went off without a hitch, and it was a lot of fun recording in the old radio station. In less than a month we were able to record six pods and had over two hundred listens and over eighteen subscribers. It was a good sign for a very organic launch. I joined as many paranormal Facebook pages as I could and promoted it as much as possible.

After a few episodes of recording the podcast inside the radio station, we had to move to another location. Another employee of the station complained to the "higher-ups" that there were "unauthorized" people (meaning John and me) inside the building after hours. Even though another manager said it was fine to record in there, we felt it best not to rock the boat, and we had to go somewhere else. At first we thought that we might have to record in Danny's basement, but something else was decided upon. Danny was a member of his local theater group in Harriston, Ontario, and had access to the building. We sat on the stage, using a wobbly table and fold-up chairs as our "recording studio". The theater was old and historic and looked very much in place along the main street of the small town. The inside was faded and musty but radiated charm, as most old buildings do. There was a very distinct energy to the place that John and I picked up on right away.

The theater was teeming with spirits, and John and I could see and sense them flitting about and moving along the rows of the seats and even up in the balcony. They would watch us with curiosity as we recorded the podcast on the stage, and they would even at times interact with us. Danny, being a bit of an expert on sound quality, suggested that we close the big heavy blue curtain on the stage to keep our voices from getting bounced back from the interior of the theater. The curtain would act as a buffer and would also serve to block out any noise from the dance studio that was in the lower level. One evening as we sat and talked about our ghostly encounters, I noticed that one section of the curtain began to move on its own right behind John. It continued for a moment and then stopped. There weren't any fans on or windows open that would allow for wind to make the curtain move. The curtain was also very heavy, and any amount of breeze to make it move would have to be quite strong. The curtain would move for us several times during random recordings.

One evening as we sat and talked, I looked to my right and behind Danny. I could see a little blond boy about eight or nine years old with a white shirt and suspenders on. He was peering from behind a side curtain right at me. I told Danny and John what I saw. Danny looked at me with a funny expression and told me that one evening a couple of years ago, he saw this same little boy on the stage in full color. He hadn't told anyone else but was fascinated that I had picked up on him and described him the same way that he had seen him. I picked up on the name Jacob, and we started calling our little pal Jake, making him our unofficial mascot. We believed that he was moving the curtains on us. He would also run around the seating area and run across the catwalk high above the seats. In one way I was glad to have him with us, but I was also sad that this little fella was grounded here for some reason, and he hadn't moved on.

Often before we recorded, I would knock on the table or on a wooden bench on the stage the *"Shave and a Haircut, Two Bits"* tune. I would leave the "two bits" part out on purpose to see if any of our ghostly theater friends would finish it for me. Several times I would do the first five knocks and have a spirit somewhere in the building finish it off with the last two knocks. We would laugh and get a kick out of it every time it happened. It gave us a positive vibe and became a tradition for us before we started the recording. Spirits routinely came to watch us record our podcast and probably wondered what these three dopes were doing on the stage, talking into an odd-looking device. We got the sense that the spirits were all older ones and from a more simple time, and the technology that we used would be very alien to them. Yet they kept appearing and let us know that they were there.

The only time we felt anything negative was one night as the three of us walked up the back stairs behind the stage, John and I felt great pressure on our chests and were winded as we got to the top. It's actually only about nine steps to get to the top and certainly not enough for either John and I to be out of breath like that. Danny wasn't affected at all. Once getting to the main stage area, I could see a huge entity, about ten feet tall, that appeared to be wearing a gray or bluish cloak walk across the left side of the stage. It actually made ripples in the air as it passed by a window that had its shades slightly open to let some light in. About ten minutes later, this same entity went in the other direction, causing the same effect in the air. John and I took the feeling of breathlessness as a negative reaction to us and believed that this massive entity was the cause. We continued to record our podcasts on stage at the theater and could always sense many spirits watching us from the seats. Often when we were recording, we would hear footsteps, odd hissing noises, see orbs of spiritual energy, and even captured EVPs on the pod. We welcomed all of it.

One night the theater was unavailable due to a play that was being rehearsed, so we had to come up with another location. Danny told us that across the street and just a little ways down was another theater called the Crown, and that the lady who owned it might let us record in there. The owner was a young woman, Raissa, who was born in Canada but had spent most of her life in the Netherlands and Spain. She was very interested in the paranormal, had a great attitude towards it, and was excited to have the podcast recorded in her building. The Crown is a very old-style theater, the kind you might see in an older film from the '50s or '60s where someone might actually escort you to your seat. It oozes nostalgia from the moment you walk in. When Raissa showed me the main auditorium of the old theater, I could see a very clear spirit of a man wearing a beige trench coat standing next to the stage. He was tall and thin and moved along the front of the first set of rows towards us before he vanished. I then looked to my left and saw a shadow person walk towards us and stand next to me. He literally looked like he was trying to nose in on our conversation. This place was crawling with spirits, and I couldn't wait to record in here.

The podcast that we were to record was with two special guests. We were having paranormal investigator Gerry Rooney and psychic medium Jen Abra on the show. The two of them had formed a ghost-hunting group called *Team Spirit – The Science Behind Spirit*. I had come across Gerry's business card at a local metaphysical shop and contacted him in the hopes that he would share his stories – to which he readily agreed. We planned to have them on the following week, and everything went smoothly.

Before every podcast, we usually meet at the local pub, have a pint or two, a snack, and discuss the topic of the evening. Usually when we are there, John and I pick up the spirit of an old man in the building. He is tall, thin, wears a black cardigan, has thick black eyebrows, and is miserable. This spirit likes to stand between the men's washroom and the kitchen or outside on the patio. When psychic medium Jen arrived, she picked up on him right away and asked what was with the miserable scowling old man in the pub. I laughed and told her that John and I were well aware of him. Immediately, the name "John" popped into my head. Moments later Jen asked me what I thought the spirit's name was. When I told her it was John, she almost choked on her drink and said that she had told Gerry and his wife, Laurie, that she also thought the spirit in the pub was named John. A nice validation for me.

Gerry, Laurie, and Jen accompanied us to the theater, and as soon as Jen walked in, she got a strong message from a spirit telling her not to come any farther into the room. She told me what she had just "heard", and I told her to tell the spirit to mind his business and move on. Jen gave me a crafty smile and kept walking. Gerry, being somewhat sensitive to spirits as well, told me he could feel and see some of the many ghosts wandering around the theater. He was grinning like a kid on Christmas day, and I was glad that he was excited to be with us that night.

John, Danny, and I set up near the stage and had Gerry and Jen sit across from us. Laurie sat off to the side and videoed us as we recorded. As we listened to their very cool paranormal stories, Jen looked just past where Danny was sitting and said she could see an old lady spirit that was floating in the air. At this same time Danny and Gerry could feel a massive cold spot form next to them. I looked to where Jen was looking, and I could briefly see the floating lady's long brownish skirt floating about a foot off the ground right in front of Gerry. John later said that none of the spirits in the theater except for this one gave him a bad vibe. We ignored the floating lady, and she moved on. Gerry then piped up and said he could sense a spirit behind him and to the right, sitting in one of the seats. I looked up and sensed a man wearing a black suit with a white shirt and black tie. It was great having other people sensing and seeing what I could see. Jen also commented on how great it was to have validations from others as well. It was an awesome podcast and a lot of fun having the two of them on the show.

SIDE NOTE: About a week later, Tony, John, Danny, and I conducted a very brief investigation of the Crown. Tony captured the full-bodied apparition of a woman walking out of the theater up the aisle on camera. John also captured several good orb pictures on his DSLR.

I always make a point of answering all the emails we receive as quickly as I can and try to be helpful as well. There are often times where listeners will ask John and I to remote view their properties, as they believe that there is something ghostly going on in their homes. It's not something that we can do all the time, but we make it a point to take on cases where children are involved. I only hope that we can continue on with the podcast for as long as we can and be as helpful as possible.

21

THE UFO

I n the autumn of 2013, my wife and I were driving home late after being at the movies. It was a clear crisp night as we traveled north on Hwy 6 from Guelph, Ontario, towards Fergus. All the leaves were already off the trees, and the scraggy silhouettes of naked trees lined the sides of the highway. There is nothing but woodlots and farm fields along the eighteen-kilometer drive other than the tiny hamlet of Ennotville. As we drove along, my wife and I noticed to our right, not more than twenty yards from the side of the road, a small thick woodlot. From the floor of the forest appeared a very large and very bright lime green sphere. It looked like someone actually flipped a switch and it came to life. The sphere was about six feet in diameter and resembled a very large beach ball. As I slowed the van down, we watched the sphere suddenly lift off the ground and rise straight up and above the canopy of the trees. It paused a moment, moved forward a few feet, and then shot like a bullet across the fields towards the east, and in a flash disappeared. We looked at each other, stunned, and collectively said, "What the hell was that?!" I am so glad that I experienced that sight with my wife, as I knew no one would believe me. Better to have another person to validate your strange experience. My only regret from that experience was that I didn't pull over and mark the spot where we saw the green sphere and come back in the morning. Perhaps the forest floor would have had burn marks or some other evidence of the odd occurrence. I haven't seen anything like it since, but I'm always watching the skies.

PHOTOS

GHOST LADY: This photo was taken by Tony from SHIP. A full apparition of a woman walking up the aisle of the Crown Harriston Theater. This location has several spirits at any given time.

FOOTPRINTS: *Two photos of the water-mark footprints that the Big John spirit left behind on John's living room floor. Their intent was to intimidate and impress. They were impressive but did nothing to intimidate me. I wear a size 15 shoe, and these prints were several inches larger and wider than mine.*

PINK APPARITION WITH LASER BEAM: When investigating Kathy's home, Michelle S of SHIP thought she heard something and decided to snap a pic on her phone. When we looked at the pic, we could see a swirling pink mist with what appears to be a laser-like orb shooting through it.

SHADOW MAN: John sent me a pic that he attempted to take of a shadow man that walked through his staircase wall. He didn't even notice the full shadow person standing in his dining room. You can actually see the brim of its hat. Could this be the Hatman that people all over the world speak of?

RENDITION OF THE GHOUL SEEN AT JOHN'S RENTAL HOME
Artwork by Dan Hammond

THE CROWN HARRISTON CULTURAL CENTRE, Photo by Dan
Hammond

WELLINGTON COUNTY MUSEUM AND ARCHIVES Photo by Dan
Hammond

22

THE NAME GAME

One "ability" I have that many other psychics, mediums, clairvoyants, etc. don't is the knack for coming up with a spirit's name. I will connect either on my own or with John, and the name of the spirit comes right to me. It's not an image in my head or a spoken word that I hear – it's just there. I can't explain it. Often when you watch the TV psychics up on stage doing their thing, they will point to a certain area of the audience and say, "Who has the strong G-sounding name?" I get the name straight up. Boom, it's there. When we were having our issues with the Big John spirit, I continually told John that his real name was Richard. John protested for a while because his own brother's name is Richard, but I insisted and said that it kept coming to me. Later on John had a strong message from one of his guides that said, "He's right." After that it was a natural talent that I had and one that I am quite proud of. I hope I don't lose the gift one day.

One time I was over at my friend and fellow investigator Corrine's home. She had joined SHIP, and after her first real investigation, I was showing her how to listen to and transcribe EVPs. As we sat in her lower-level family room, I could see to my right a spirit out of the corner of my eye. Another was moving behind Corrine as she sat in her chair at the computer. I looked to the spirit to my right. "Who is Harold?" Corrine looked at me, a little perplexed, and said that was her uncle.

"And Reginald? Who is that?" I asked. Another uncle, she told me. These were two very uncommon names, and they were both related to her. They were both in the room with us. Another name came to me. "Your father is passed?" She confirmed that he was. "His name starts with a J?" Corrine just looked at me, a little wide eyed, and said that it did indeed start with a J. I got excited. "Is it John? Jim?" She replied no, and I stopped myself. I was getting too cocky and excited, and I wasn't listening. "His name is Jerry," I said. Corrine looked at me, and her eyes started to get a little glassy. His actual name was Gerald, but he went by Jerry, she told me. Wow. I was on a roll tonight.

During the time that I was showing Corrine how to use the audio program on her computer, I had asked her about her own paranormal experiences. She told me that recently she had been finding dimes in the most random places. She said that she had even found one in a coffee shop on her table and knew that it was there for her. Corrine's sister had passed away in the past two years, and for some reason she felt that the coffee shop dime was from her. I took a picture of the room and sent it to John to see what he could pick up on. He messaged me back right away. "Is she finding dimes all over the place?" he texted. Wow. Bang on again. Corrine was blown away. At the same time that John had messaged me back, I got a very clear image of her deceased father, Jerry. I described him to her: An older man in his seventies, thin, gray slick-backed hair. Lots of Brylcreem. He was wearing glasses and a thick gray cardigan, the type with the really thick collars. Corrine confirmed that was her father to a tee. John messaged me again to tell Corrine that her father and the two uncles had presented themselves to him, and they wanted her to know that the dimes were from them, but the one "out in the open" (coffee shop) was from her sister. Corrine did a great job of holding it together. It was an emotional experience. As we sat there and I told her more about John's amazing talents, I had another name come to me. "Who is Steve?" I asked. Corrine said that she had a cousin Steve staying with her for a while, but she also had an Uncle Steve who had passed on. "And Helen?" I asked. "Who is that?" Corrine confirmed that was a deceased aunt. It was a veritable family reunion in her family room, and I was the greeter.

Not long after the visit to Corrine's home, I was messaged by Michelle of SHIP and asked if I could come to her friend Janet's house. Janet and her husband were doing major renovations at their place, and since they had started, they were getting a strong sense of something in their basement. It was such a strong feeling that when they went downstairs, they wouldn't turn their head towards a certain area for fear of what they might see standing there. I arrived at Janet's home and brought my K2 meter with me. I messaged John and told him what was going on. He and I both got strong images of bare wood framing and insulation.

I arrived at the home and walked into the mother of all renovations. Janet's entire main floor was gutted. The kitchen, dining area, and living room were nothing but framed walls, insulation, exposed pipes, wiring, and assorted junk all over the place. There wasn't any lighting, and they were using battery-powered lamps and candles. There were a couple of lawn chairs to sit on and not much else.

Janet and her husband told me about the presence in the basement and the strong feeling of being watched when they went down there. Michelle's teenage son, Jerrod, was with us and was having his own experiences with some clairvoyant gifts that he was sorting out.

Michelle and I went down to the basement to see what we could pick up on. The basement was jam-packed with boxes, trinkets, DVDs, books, furniture from upstairs and anything else you could think of. There was so much stuff down there that they had to make aisles through the chaos to get to different parts of the room. I had to turn sideways to maneuver my way through. I took my K2 meter out and spoke to the room. I could definitely feel that an unseen energy was there with us. "If there is someone here with us, can you please touch this K2 meter and make it light up for us?" I asked. I set the meter down on top of a box. Nothing. The lights didn't blink at all. I asked again several times. Still nothing. We told the spirit that we knew it was there and it was welcome to communicate with us. Still nothing. Then a name came to me. I looked at Michelle. "Is there anyone connected to Janet by the name of Ron?" I asked. Michelle had no idea and shrugged her shoulders. After a few more minutes we went back upstairs. "Is there someone in your life who is connected to you by the name of Ron?" I asked Janet. She gave me a puzzled look and shook her head. Nope.

Jerrod and I then went downstairs to see if he could pick up on something. Jerrod could immediately feel the strong presence down there. We could both see a bit of a shadowy spirit and followed it with our eyes as it moved to different spots around the room. After a few moments, we retreated up the stairs. As soon as I hit the top step, I locked eyes with Janet. She slapped her forehead and said, "Holy shit, Ron! I know who Ron is!" Ron and his wife were friends of Janet's, and he had passed on not too long ago. After he was gone, his wife was stuck with all of his belongings and wanted to clear out some room at her place and started giving some of Ron's possessions away to friends and family. Apparently Janet had ended up with some of Ron's things, including some of his mother's personal belongings, such as an old antique washboard. The problem was that

Ron's belongings were buried under a ton of other things in the basement, and he was NOT happy about it. Before Jerrod and I left the basement, I sent a picture of the room to John. He texted me and said that it was an older gentleman, and he was pissed that the house was under renovations because, according to Ron, there was nothing wrong with the house the way it was. Ron kept repeating this to John over and over. I spoke to the air in the room to address Ron. I told him that the house would be back to normal soon enough and that his belongings would get the respect they deserved. Janet and her husband were good with the spirit now since they knew who it was. As I stood there, something came to me. I asked Janet, "Did Ron work with his hands?" He had, she said. "A machinist?" I asked. Yes, she confirmed. "Tool and die," I said. Janet and her husband looked at me with some amazement. I looked at Michelle, and she was grinning from ear to ear. She was impressed with what I was able to pick up on. Janet then confirmed that they had some of Ron's tool and die equipment, "Somewhere in the basement." I then described Ron to Janet, and she confirmed that I was bang on.

As I left their home, I felt good about what I was just able to do. Things were changing for me, and my intuition was getting sharper. I was learning how to "listen to spirit" and use the gifts that I had to help others.

Another time that I was able to use my name game "party trick" was when I was recording some voice work at a studio in Kitchener, Ontario. My filmmaker friend Rob was working on directing a series of short films where I got to play a hit man named McMillan. McMillan was my father's middle name, and I asked Rob to make it my character's name, to which he quickly agreed. The studio had a definite energy to it, and I knew that I would see something eventually. It wasn't long before the ghosts came out to see what we were all up to.

The studio had at least three spirits in it that I could figure out. While talking with one of the employees named Michael, he told me that he also believed there were spirits in the building. Michael said that he had seen one once and had had others tell him that they could see things move on their own in the studio. As we spoke, a name came to me. "Who is Edward?" I asked. Michael looked at me and shrugged. He had no idea. He then texted the actual owner of the studio and asked the question. Minutes later Michael's phone beeped, and after reading the response, he turned in his chair and looked at me wide eyed. He told me that the owner's father's name was Edward. Michael had goosebumps up and down his forearms. Another name came to me. "Who is Patty? Or Patricia?" Michael quickly sent another text. Once again, he looked at his phone and turned to me to pass on the replying message. "Patty was Edward's first wife!" The other actors and support people in the room turned and looked at me. They couldn't believe what I had come up with. The questions started coming at me almost immediately. I told them that I had no idea why I was so good with spirits' names. They didn't project to me; they didn't say a spoken word to me; they just appeared as a thought. It was something that I was still trying to figure out for myself.

As we sat there watching some of the other actors record some voice-overs in the studio, I looked at the doorway to one of the other rooms and could see a spirit standing in the doorway. He was thin, wore glasses, and had a mustache. I told Michael about the spirit. He told me that a gentleman by the name of Ron had passed away the year prior and that the doorway that I had seen him standing in had been his office. The others in the room looked at the doorway and then back at me. One of the girls there joked that I was the *"ghost whisperer"*. I then looked over at a framed photo on one of the walls. It was the man whom I had seen in spirit form. I told Michael that this was the person I had seen. I came to realize that my talent for coming up with the names of spirits was when I was in a comfortable setting and mood. It was easier for me to get "in the zone" and listen to what was being projected to me. As I was leaving the building, I looked down one of the halls only to see a male and female spirit watching me. This was obviously Edward and Patty. I gave them a smile and quick nod and left.

23

BUD AND EARL

I n the summer of 2018, as my ghostly adventures (and misadventures) became more commonplace, I often wondered about what spirit guides I might have had around me. John was told by a lady with considerable clairvoyant gifts that he had eight guides around him and one was actually nonhuman. She told him that he had a hawk as one of his guides. John told me that he had actually felt that he had eight around him but was only at the time aware of three. One was a man from Nova Scotia named Gerry, an old female family friend they called Burrel, and a native man that he couldn't figure his connection to. Spirit guides are apparently around us all the time (according to the experts) and, in the world of mediums, psychics and clairvoyants, play a large role in our spiritual endeavors.

When I was just a kid, maybe eleven or twelve years old, I can remember lying on the family room floor, doing some drawing. The phone rang in the adjacent room, and I heard my dad answer it. Moments later, I could hear him become very emotional, and he slammed the phone down with his hand. Concerned for my father, as he never acted this way, I sat up and started toward the other room where the phone was. My mom met me before I was able to enter the room and told me that my uncle Bud had died. This was probably the first time in my life up to this point that I had experienced a loss of a family member. My uncle was a great lovable man who always treated my sister and me very well. He had apparently suffered a heart attack while driving, left the road, and crashed into a railroad embankment. I believe that he was pronounced dead at the scene.

My uncle's wife – my aunt Ruth – was now alone in their beautiful home in Halton Hills. A short time after the funeral, my parents and I went to visit her. My aunt Ruth was known by many of the family to be a very spiritual woman. She was very quiet at times but always had interesting stories to tell. It was also well known that her home was very haunted; she was very receptive to the spirits and welcomed their presence. The home that they lived in had been built on an actual American Indian burial ground. They'd discovered this by accident as they had begun to make some improvements in their backyard and, upon digging, found American Indian plates, bowls, and other important artifacts. They did the right thing and stopped digging. The University of Toronto was called, and a team of archaeologists conducted a dig. American Indian elders, I believe, were also called in so that the findings would be cared for properly and archived. Right after this was when things became interesting in their home and on the property.

My aunt and uncle's son, Rick, headed down to the basement one evening to get some beer from the bar fridge. On his way back upstairs with an armload of bottles, an old American Indian woman suddenly appeared before him. Her rapid appearance and look of anger caused Rick to yell out, throw his arms up, and run down the stairs and out the back door. The beer bottles crashed to the ground, and the old American Indian woman faded away. On another occasion, Rick was lying on the basement couch, watching television, when suddenly the couch, with him on it, was lifted off the ground and was slammed back and forth with great force. Rick was able to scramble off the couch and fled as fast as he could. My aunt told me that they would often hear footsteps running down the hall at night and that she'd actually captured the chants and beating of drums coming from the woods behind their home on audiotape. There were many more incidents that happened in the home, but I wasn't fortunate enough at the time to hear all the stories.

One other story that I was told came from my cousin Chris (their grandson). He was at my uncle and aunt's home for a weekend visit when he was eight or nine years old. While they were all sitting on the couch, talking, Chris suddenly noticed something moving on the coffee table in front of them. As he looked with more attention, he saw what appeared to be a tiny, action-figure-sized person peering from behind a candle holder or some other kind of knickknack. Chris pointed at the small humanoid creature and asked his grandparents what the heck it was. Apparently, they could also see the same thing and told him just to forget about it and ignore it. The little person then darted across the table and hid behind another item on the coffee table. It's something that he will never forget and never be able to fully explain. The fact that my aunt and uncle were aware of the tiny creature's presence, and their cavalier attitude towards it, made me think and wonder what other strange things were associated with their home and property.

During a visit to my aunt after my uncle's funeral, we all sat in the living room. My dad and I sat on a couch against a main wall, and across from us was my mom and my aunt in wingback chairs with a beautiful stone fireplace between them. Being a young kid at the time – and way before electronic devices – I was entertaining myself at the coffee table with some paper and drawing supplies. I looked up from my artwork, and behind my aunt was a large wood box for the fireplace. Sitting on the box was a very surly-looking American Indian woman. She was very clear to me and, to this day, one of the clearest spirits I have ever seen. I immediately told everyone that I could see her. My aunt smiled at me and said that she knew that she was there. She explained that she was the nasty spirit that had scared their son, Rick, half to death. I then looked over at my mom and could see my uncle Bud standing behind her chair. He too came across very clear to me but not as clear as the angry-looking American Indian woman. I announced to the room that I could see my uncle. My mom looked at me with wide eyes and said that she could feel him standing behind her, as he was giving her wicked goosebumps up her arms and back. My aunt could also see her recently deceased husband and didn't show any signs of it bothering her one bit. It was almost like she had expected him to be there, and the fact that he was a ghostly presence wasn't a problem at all.

My aunt, as I said, was a very quiet woman and to me was hard to approach on the topic of spirits. The subject enthralled me at the time, and I wished that I had taken the time to learn more from her. She let my mom know that she knew many of the American Indian spirits in her home and on the property. There were several good ones that looked out for her and several that were quite unpleasant, such as the old woman who had terrorized my cousin Rick. Now her husband was added to the ghostly equation and was a spirit for good in the home.

My uncle Earl (Bud's brother) was the one uncle that I probably saw the least, but when I did, it was always a fun time. He used to have a crazy little dog called Brutus that was fearless. I would roll a ball down our stone stairs leading to the basement, and the dog would tear down to retrieve it. I did this over and over until I came up with an idea. I tossed the ball over the landing instead of rolling it down the stairs, thinking the dog would run around the railing and go down the stairs after the ball. Instead, the little nutcase jumped over the landing and flew through the air and crashed down on the stone steps. My uncle nearly had a heart attack and thought that the dog had committed doggy suicide. Moments later Brutus came trotting up the stairs, wagging his tail, with the ball in his mouth without a scratch on him. Tough dog for a tough uncle.

Earl had been (as was my uncle Bud) a World War II veteran. He had served his time in Italy and, during the course of the war, had been shot three times on three different occasions. Once in the back, once in the leg, and once in the head. After he returned home, he had often verbally announced his dislike for Italians after fighting them all the time, so it was only natural that one day he married one. Go figure. He had a thick frame, an army-style flat-top haircut, and didn't take any shit from anyone. Once while walking through a forest back home in Canada, a bullet whizzed past his head. Being a seasoned war veteran, he took cover and waited for the second shot to come. When it didn't, he looked out from cover and saw an Italian man with a hunting rifle walking towards him. Apparently the man mistook him for a deer and took a shot. The hunter pretended that he didn't speak any English, hoping that Earl would understand and not do anything rash. My uncle then laid him out with a blow to the jaw. Probably didn't help that the guy was an Italian either...

Many years later, Earl became ill with terminal cancer. Instead of going through endless amounts of treatments, multiple hospital visits, and whatever other nasty business comes with the disease, he opted to go out quickly and ended his own life. This was quite upsetting to his family and to his many brothers and sisters, but eventually they accepted his decision and honored him by drinking their fill at his wake.

One night while sitting at home, completing some artwork, I received a text from John. He told me that three spirits – two men and a woman – had appeared before him, and for some reason he knew they were connected to me. I immediately knew that one of them was my uncle Bud. John said that the man had a great smile and was reflecting that to him. John then described the lady spirit to me in the best way that he could. He told me that he couldn't get a clear image of her but sensed that she was a quiet lady, but when she spoke, everyone listened. This described my aunt Ruth to a tee. She had passed away a few years earlier, and I felt bad, as I wasn't able to attend her memorial. I ran upstairs and took a picture of my uncle Bud and Aunt Ruth's photo with my cell phone and sent them to John. He replied to the picture of my uncle, "Yep! That's him. There's that smile!" He couldn't get a clear image of the other man but said that he was stocky and seemed like the kind of person who wouldn't take any shit from anyone. I knew right then and there that it was my uncle Earl. John strongly felt that they were presenting themselves to him so that he would let me know that they were looking in on me from time to time. I couldn't be happier having the three of them "floating" around my place and wished that I could communicate with them at a different level. The three of them were to be my spirit guides, and my two uncles would be instrumental in helping John and I rid homes of unwanted spirits.

24

GOSHEN, INDIANA

I became a part of several paranormal Facebook pages in the summer of 2018. My intention was mostly to promote the podcast and get it out there for people to see and listen to. I wasn't interested in seeing endless pictures of dust and bugs floating through people's homes and them asking everyone else what they thought of the ghostly "orbs" that were visiting them. There are far too many people who interpret the slightest sound or odd sensation as being paranormal. I would quickly scan through these pages and then began not to look at them at all.

One page did stand out from all the others though. It was a page designed to assist people who were having "real" issues with possibly paranormal activity and were seeking help from others. The Facebook page had many psychics and mediums who would offer to help the people who were seemingly at their wits' end. One of them was a lady named "Kate".

Kate was a single mom and lived in a small modest two-story home that was in the rough part of town. She said that the police were constantly at her neighbors' homes, and there was a lot of drug use in the area. To add to her residential woes, Kate stated that she was hearing footsteps and banging on her stairs and on the walls of her home. She would get unexplained cold spots in the home, and her cat would react to things that weren't there. Her toddler son would also wake up every night at exactly 9:30, screaming bloody terror, and would tear at her to pick him up when she came in to see what was wrong with him. Kate also said there were feelings of unease in the home, and she could sense something around her at times. John and I made an unofficial pact that when we saw anything where a child was involved, then we would try our best to help.

I asked Kate to send me some photos of where the activity was the most prevalent. She quickly sent pics of her son's bedroom, playroom, and the doorway to her basement. She was quite trusting towards someone she didn't even know. I chalked this up to her fear and desperation in finding help. As usual, I forwarded the pics to John. As I sent them, I got a strong sensation that we were dealing with a female spirit. John did his thing and quickly got back to me. In one of the pictures of the boy's bedroom was a black blanket draped over the existing drapes. Kate said it was to make the room darker for when the baby slept. John had an image of a hand shaking the blanket in order to scare the child. He also told me that something would shake his crib to terrorize him as well. John messaged me again and said that the spirit was "quite a bitch". He could also see a child spirit there and a male spirit in the background. When I had sent the series of pictures, John told me that the picture with the black blanket hadn't come through until later on. It was the first picture I had sent to him. He felt that it was the female spirit trying to show her power and blocked the photo to keep John from picking up on the black blanket. John requested that the blanket be removed for now so it couldn't be used to scare the baby.

I messaged Kate and told her what John had said about the blanket. Kate told me that it was the blanket that the baby was actually born on. She also told me that she was told that she would never get pregnant, and he was her little "miracle baby". She put it away for now and continued to trust us. As I messaged Kate about what we were planning on doing, I told her that the spirit was an older lady and not some demonic entity out of a bad horror movie. I then asked Kate where she was located. I had presumed that she was in Ontario and possibly not far from either John or me. She then told me that she lived in Goshen, Indiana. *Holy cow! I wasn't expecting that at all.* I had been able to slightly remote view homes within an hour or two's drive from me, but Indiana was something like a ten-hour trek from where I lived. I also certainly wasn't expecting to be assisting someone in the USA. I messaged John and told him where she was from. "Distance means nothing," he messaged back. "We could probably help someone as far away as Australia."

I tried my best to view the home. As I stood in what I believed to be the baby's room, I could see a very short and tiny-framed old woman walk in with her hands clasped in front of her. She had moppy brownish gray hair, a black long-sleeved shirt with a floral print, and an ugly gray ankle-length skirt. This was the "bitch" that John could detect. She seemed to be in her own little world and shuffled her way into the room. I tried my best to envision this woman in light so that she might stop and I could reason with her somehow. She ignored me, and I lost track of her. John did his best at interacting with her as well but had no luck. She was in her own little world and acted like she couldn't even see that we were there. I couldn't even pick up on her name, as she was so closed off to us. Her sole purpose was to torment that poor child and cause anxiety and grief for the mother. Over the next hour John and I tried our best to contain her and move her from the home. I was having major issues even seeing where she was, and it was almost like something was blocking me. I felt useless this time around. As John and I communicated via text messages, our thumbs felt like they were going to fall off, so we decided to switch to a voice call. As we spoke, our phones both dropped the calls. We tried again to call each other several times, but our phones stopped working. We both had full signal strength, but the phones wouldn't work. This malicious woman was somehow affecting our phones and keeping us from speaking. All the lights in John's home dimmed for a few seconds as well as she tried to absorb some energy. This was a good sign, according to John though. This meant that she was fearful of us and whatever we were planning was going to work.

John was able to get images of babies around her and said that she had had several miscarriages back in the day and was miserable in life due to the fact that she could never have children. The fact that Kate's little guy was born a "miracle baby" angered her even more. For whatever reason she wanted to take her anger and frustration out on Kate's son. He also received a message that she would be a tough nut to crack but would eventually wear down, and we could move her soon enough.

The next day I found some quiet time, got comfortable, and focused on the house. An older lady friend of mine once taught me a good way to help to clear homes of negative energy. You envision a tiny little marble-sized shiny "disco ball" in the home and enlarge it slowly. Its reflective surface repels the dark energy as it gets bigger and bigger. Eventually the ball is so big that it engulfs the entire home. As it grows, it fills itself with bright white protective light. I did this in the home and felt good about it. John messaged me later and told me that he did the same thing and filled the home with white light. I checked my phone. It was 10:00 p.m. I hadn't heard from Kate. She said 9:30 p.m. was the "witching hour" at her home, as that was when the activity would ramp up and the baby would wake up screaming. The next day I checked my phone and received a message from her. *"That was a great night!!!"* (Add happy face.)

I kept up communication with Kate over the next few days and made sure that all was well. She said the home felt good, and she was happy that the spirit was gone. This had been an easy home to clear. I thought that we would have had to do more to move the old lady spirit, but I supposed that she wasn't up for a fight and quickly gave in and moved on. I just hope that she found her peace and hasn't moved on to another home to torment someone else.

25

QUEENSLAND, AUSTRALIA

G'day, mate! This story is a fairly quick one compared to some of the others. I offered John a theory that I believed that a lot of the spirits that we were coming across and ended up moving wanted to be moved. A lot of them lacked the confidence or reason to move along on their own. Ghostly procrastinators, if you will. One such case was the spirit in Queensland, Australia.

A young lady reached out to one of the Facebook pages and was looking for help in relation to a poltergeist that she thought she had in her home. A gaming controller was thrown at a guest in her hallway, her brother's mattress kept getting flipped over, and her brother saw the spirit of a young man inside the house. The spirit projected himself as having a burnt face and had a fork sticking out of his eye. Ouch. I contacted this young woman and told her that we could help her with her problem. We requested some photos of the inside of the home to work from and went about remote viewing as best we could. From Canada to Australia in seconds. If only...

As soon as I had sent the pics to John, he had the spirit visit him in his own home. I could then see this spirit as a young teen, approximately fifteen to seventeen years old, slim with short brown hair. He was wearing a red T-shirt. John confirmed his appearance, and he tried his best to communicate with him. The teen was silent, had "dead eyes", and quickly moved on. John said that there was an older male spirit with him, and he believed that it was the younger spirit's father. The father was trying his best to get his son to move on with him but was being ignored. I explained to John that I believed that the spirit felt "distant" and had some possible mental health issues.

I messaged Australia and asked her if she'd had anyone pass along in her life who suffered from mental health issues. She said that her brother was ill and that he had just been released from a mental health hospital. She also added that a young man died one floor above him when he was there. John and I believed that this newly deceased spirit had followed her brother to his home.

Things were busy for John and me over the next couple of days. Other than life getting in the way, we were now getting requests from other people to help them rid their homes of spirits. Queensland got ignored for a couple of days, and I felt bad that we hadn't taken care of things sooner. The lady there said that the activity was continuing, and she was getting quite upset. All of the previous times that a spirit was moved was when John and I would team up and go move them. I wondered if this time, I could do it myself. I sat down in my recliner, quieted myself, and focused on the Aussie home. Soon, I could see the young man standing there next to me. He never gave me his name or made any eye contact. I placed my hands on his shoulders and gave my usual pep talk about moving on, not being judged, etc. I had also asked my two uncles, Earl and Bud, to assist me just in case. I sensed the young spirit's father appear. He was quiet and very reserved and almost seemed to walk on eggshells around his son. Moments later I felt an odd but good sensation and had a feeling that the house was now cleared.

Once again I messaged the young lady and asked what the feeling was like in the house. She told me that nothing out of the ordinary was going on, and she felt that we had been successful in clearing the home. I told her that she was to message me if anything else happened. So far, so good.

26

WHERE THE HELL IS GOD...?

I must confess that I do not believe in Jesus Christ, the Prophet Mohammad, Buddha, Krishna, or any of the other 3,500 or so Gods and deities that have worshipers all over the globe. I was christened in a Protestant church when I was a baby but, other than the odd wedding or funeral, never set foot in a house of worship. You can say that I am not much of a believer.

I once belonged to a Christian youth group in high school but only because there were some good-looking girls in it, and we played a lot of baseball. I didn't stay long though. We were having an outing in a local park, and I can actually remember the moment I quit the group when our church leader came over and pointed out a young couple picnicking with their newborn baby. He told us that he was speaking with them and had been told by the parents that the baby hadn't been baptized yet, so if it died, it would immediately be sent to Hell for all eternity. All the other kids nodded in agreement and cast their gaze at the couple with judgment in their eyes. I thought that was lunacy and decided right then and there that I didn't want to be a part of something that would cast a beautiful innocent baby into a lake of fire just because some dude didn't sprinkle water on its head. Besides, the good Christian girls weren't putting out...

I am willing to admit, though, that in the past couple of years, I am more willing to suggest that there is something out there. My mind is expanding, and my horizons are broadening. I find myself being open to more and more celestial and other-worldly things. I just dismiss the idea that there is a bearded man sitting on a throne, greeting people as they pass through the pearly gates, and I am more apt to think that everything around us, including the infinite universe, is "God". An energy that certainly doesn't interfere in our affairs and sits quietly by to observe or ignore.

One of the questions I often have in relation to the para-normal is, if you were an asshole in life, then why are you permitted to continue to be an asshole in death? Take the case of Big John, for example, or the spirit that terrorized me as a child. Who is minding or policing the afterlife? Where is the all-knowing omnipotent grand master that rewards the good and punishes evil? Big John was taken away by other good spirits into "the light", yet the colossal douchebag was able to return and continue his antics on a new family. How was this allowed? Could it be that there are many more levels of the afterlife than we know of and the light that we send them to is not the final destination? Did Big John make a deal with another power out there in the great beyond to return, or did he do it on his own? So many questions and not many answers.

The problem that I have found is that there is never a common denominator among the clairvoyant communities. One psychic will tell you that she doesn't believe in demons and that Satan only lives at church as an icon of control. Another will tell you that demons are absolutely real and that Satan sends them to wreak havoc topside. Who do you believe? One lady who clears homes remotely swears to me that demons aren't real and that they are actually aliens who come here via dimensional portals to feed off our energy. So many experienced "experts" and so many varying thoughts and opinions. I wonder if we will ever know for certain. Maybe aliens and demons co-exist and use the same portals and wormholes to conduct their business. It makes my head ache thinking about it and trying to make sense of it all.

As John and I encounter more and more dark nonhuman entities in our paranormal travels, I wonder where they come from and, again – who allows them to exist? Are they actually demons? John and I came to think for a short period of time that the so-called "demons" were actually old earthbound spirits that figured out how to use their energy to portray themselves as something frightening. Their reasons are known only to them, and one can only speculate as to their intentions. Boredom?

Tony from SHIP, when conducting EVPs, will often ask the spirits if Jesus Christ is their Lord and Savior. After eight years of him asking, he has never received an answer. Are the spirits forbidden somehow from answering, or do they just not know? One medium friend of mine said very matter-of-factly, "I think that when people die, a lot of them are going to be really, really surprised." She herself, I believe, is nonreligious yet believes in a higher power. Just not the one they teach you on Sundays.

John and I have encountered several spirits who believed that if they moved on and into the light, they would be judged and punished in Hell. The spirit from the Clifford home believed this, and that's why he never moved on. He had been deceased for almost twenty years but wandered aimlessly, looking for things in death that he never had in life.

When we are able to, we calm spirits down and communicate with them as human beings. We tell them that they will be fine once they move on and they won't be judged. This is not an actual absolute for me because I just don't know, and might never know, until the fateful day when I kick the bucket. I just believe that it's true and use it in my bag of tricks. I have been successful enough to convince many of them that they will be fine, and they trust me enough to go. I hope that I haven't sold them false hope. I am assuming for now that we have only encountered spirits that when they were alive were brought up in Christian homes. I am only basing this on the geography and demographics of some of the places that we have remotely projected to. It would be interesting to come across an earth-bound spirit that was raised Buddhist or Sikh.

Often spirits will be trapped and confused in whatever plane of existence they are in. They wander throughout homes, businesses, and parks, looking for something that will make them happy and content again. Their frustration growing as the living (most of them at least) can't see them or communicate with them when they want to. The spirits figure out how to manipulate matter and move objects or manifest into images that frighten people. Many of the spirits that needed to be moved that John and I came into contact with had suffered from mental health issues when they were alive, and this seemed to carry on to their death. The case of the Hamilton poltergeist or the Queensland spirit are good examples of this. The notion that they were still suffering in death is a hard thing to take. Shouldn't their troubles have ended for them in the afterlife? Where is the fairness in that? Where is the all-loving deity to guide them on to a better place?

Another thing to consider is the fact that John and I don't use religion to move the spirits. We don't wander around the house sprinkling holy water and shouting, "The power of Christ compels you!" We basically walk around physically or astrally and say, "Get the fuck out of here, you meathead!" Don't laugh, it works. Not all the time, but so far we have a good track record.

As a certainty, I can tell you that aliens are real, and we are not alone in the universe. I have come face-to-face with Greys in their astral form and have seen a UFO. I began to wonder though, do they worship an all-knowing omnipotent God? Do they have a Jesus figure to worship and a book that many of them use to live their lives by? Many people believe them to be here for nefarious reasons and use poor unfortunate people as lab experiments. The more I read up on them and listen to other people's own encounters with them, the more I think that might be true. I just hope that there are some other alien species that are out there in our corner and are looking out for us.

Michelle Desrochers and an anonymous friend of hers both remote viewed John's property upon request. John was having issues with tons of shadow people, a white translucent being with a head shaped like a Tic Tac, and other oddities. It was affecting someone in the home, and he was looking for help with something that was beyond his abilities. Michelle and her friend did their "thing" and got back to me quickly. Michelle said it was pretty bad and that there was much, much more going on at John's place than he knew about.

Michelle told us that there was a massive portal in the back of John's property, and it was so big that she couldn't see the top of it. She could hear screaming coming from it and the sound of crackling fire. Inside his home was a small reptilian being about four feet tall and some ghastly thing that crawled up the walls, which had a doglike body but had another set of limbs and a nasty squished face with tiny razor-like teeth.

Michelle called upon her spirit guides and rounded up these monstrosities by trapping them in light and sending them through a small portal that she created. The final thing she encountered was a large black snakelike creature under John's home that her guides dealt with and removed. Unfortunately, according to Michelle, the portal behind his home could not be closed. It was amazing that she had mentioned this portal in the back of John's place, as he had hooked up a motion-sensitive trail cam in his backyard and often captured odd images. The pics that John captured ranged from large glowing anomalies, laser-like beams of light going through the trees, and bizarre orbs.

Michelle stated that the portal's massive size and the power emanating from it made it nearly impossible to deal with. Before leaving John's home in her "astral" form, she surrounded his place in a ball of bright light in the hopes that nothing could get in. The next day John told me that while he and his significant other slept, they were woken by a loud and heavy bang on the roof of the home. It happened a couple of times and almost sounded like something was pounding in frustration on the roof because it couldn't get in.

Hearing all of this had my head spinning again. It made me think of the realities of the world and how many unknown "things" were out there that the average person just had no clue about. It also made me think about the existence of God again. Why was this portal and its dark secrets allowed to remain? The screaming coming from within – who were they, and why wasn't anyone doing something to help them? When I asked Michelle about them, she quietly said that they may be lost souls that became trapped within. Was there no one with the knowledge or abilities to help them? Why wasn't some evil prick like Big John in there with them?

When I was much younger, in my teens, I came across a psychic medium and asked her about what happened to people who committed suicide. At the time I was worried for my uncle Earl's "soul" and wanted to hear something positive from her. This lady told me that suicides were all in a *"deep well of despair"* and that no light could reach them. They stayed in a constant state of confusion and were unreachable. This didn't make me feel any better about my uncle, and I hoped that she was wrong.

I know now that he is all well and good in the spirit realm and hope that he is happy.

The topic of death and the afterlife can weigh heavily on some people. We all fear death, but all want to go to "Heaven" if there is such a place. We have all heard tales of people on their death beds claiming to see their long-deceased relatives waiting for them, bathed in light. Then heard the stories of people having near-death experiences and being sucked down into a black hole by demonic hands, only to be given a second chance at life and a chance at redemption. Then there are the spirits who linger willingly or unwillingly, either content to remain or too afraid to move on. Who makes the rules? So many questions and never a straight answer.

27

THE GHOUL

M aria, of the Oakville investigation, messaged John and told him that she was experiencing more problems and issues with malicious "things" in her basement apartment. Entities were entering her home, talking to her, leaving noxious odors in the home, and her young son was complaining of being "bitten" as he slept. Maria was a virtual magnet for spirits, and even with this knowledge and knowing that her antenna was up, she continued to try to communicate with spirits and would visit "haunted" locations. John warned her several times to leave well enough alone, but she ignored him. Her compulsion to visit scary locations was stronger than John's advice.

Maria visited a very old, and now defunct, boarded-up mental health facility in the Hamilton, Ontario, area. She wandered the grounds, took pictures of it, and – although I can't be certain – probably tried to conduct some EVP sessions while there. Visiting this place was one of the things that John had warned her about, but her personal obsession with the para-normal overwhelmed her, and she gave in. She texted John and told him that she was smelling what appeared to be ammonia and rotten eggs in her place. John didn't remote view her place as he (and I) often brought home more than we bargained for. He gave her advice on protecting herself for the one-thousandth time and left it for the time being. A day or so later, John awoke at roughly three in the morning to something that hammered him in the chest so bad that he bolted upright and sprang from the bed. He stated that it had felt almost like when the Big John spirit would strike him as he slept. His chest right back to his spine hurt so bad that he took powerful painkillers to become comfortable again. At first John thought that it was something that had followed him home from his rental property. He and his better half had been vigorously renovating, painting, and making minor repairs to the home in the hopes of putting it on the market. John would often tell me that he felt heavy presences in the rental as he worked on things and assumed that the spirits that still inhabited the place were pissed at the activity in the home.

A couple of days later John messaged me and said that he had a very strong feeling that whatever had *"smoked him in the chest"* was the "thing" from Maria's place and not from the rental home. He assumed that it was angry and possibly slightly intimidated by John. It most likely didn't care for his communication with Maria and had paid him a visit in hopes of scaring him off.

The next day after returning from the gym early in the morning, I lay back down on the bed for a rest. The past couple of nights I had had unpleasant dreams, restless sleeps, and was always worn out. The moment I lay down and closed my eyes, I received a very clear image of John walking through the kitchen of his rental property. He was wearing a white ball cap and an orange- and rust-colored golf shirt. My eyes popped open, and I texted him right away, asking him if he was in his kitchen just a moment ago. John confirmed that he had just walked through the space. I then asked him if he was wearing the cap and golf shirt, which he confirmed. I was blown away for a moment. I had remote viewed John in his rental home, saw what he was wearing, and it had all been in full color and real time. John then told me that he saw a "ghoulish"-looking shadow man in the home, which had pointed ears, elongated fingers, and was hunched over. It was affecting him and making him feel angry and aggressive.

I messaged John back and said that I would do a "disco ball" of protection to see if it would help. I closed my eyes and found myself in the living room off the kitchen. Just as I started to conjure the ball, I looked over at the stairs leading up to the upper level and saw this ghoul that John spoke of. It was about four steps up from the bottom and was looking upstairs. It was dark gray in color, was slightly hunched forward, had a long pointy chin, a pointy topped head, and seriously long fingers. I formed the ball of protection quickly and pushed it out the far wall. At the time of this writing, neither John nor I have seen it again.

28

JACK

My neighbors asked my teenage daughter to look after their house cats during the Christmas holidays, as they would be away for two weeks visiting family. All she was required to do was go in every day, feed, and water the cats, and maybe give them a scratch or two behind the ears. Everything went well until she came back home after feeding the cats and took me aside to ask me a couple of questions. She told me that while she was feeding the cats, she could see movement out of the corner of her eye. She would turn to see what was there only to find nothing at all. She then stated that she saw what appeared to be an "orb" float across the dining room. She quickly left the neighbors' and came home. As someone who sees spirits everywhere, I didn't get bothered by this and ignored it. I assumed that at least one of my kids would be sensitive to spirits like their old man. My daughter continued to look after the cats, and everything went well.

A day or two later, my daughter came home to find some objects in her room had been moved from their permanent spots to other locations in her room. A figure had been moved from the top of a shelf to the middle of the floor, and some random items on her makeup desk were not in the same spot as she left them. A little voice in the back of my head said, *"Uh-oh,"* but I downplayed it as much as I could. She was still a little freaked out by what she'd seen at the neighbors', and I figured her mind was playing tricks on her. In my gut, I knew that something paranormal was going on. The next day she came home again and found two foam toy swords that had been placed in the back of her closet now leaning against her bedroom window. They belonged to her younger brother, and I had put them in his sister's closet to give me a reprieve from endless sword fights and me getting whacked with them. When we asked him if he had moved them, he said that he hadn't, and I believed him. I asked John for help.

I sent John a couple of pics of my daughter's room for him to remotely view. John then told me that there was a young male, maybe fourteen years old, dressed in '40s-style clothes, who had followed my daughter home from the neighbors'. He had been the shadow in the corner of her eye and the orb that floated across the room. John believed him to be harmless, and his moving objects was just to get my daughter's attention. John communicated with the kid and told him that he had to knock it off or there would be problems for him. The kid then disappeared, and the activity in my daughter's room ended.

John messaged me a couple of days later and told me that the kid spirit was popping in and out at his place. John was frustrated because the kid kept turning John's TV off on him when he was watching it. John finally had it and "pushed" the kid out with protective light. John messaged me again...In the message was a picture of John's car out in his driveway with the trunk popped wide open. John said that the kid – out of spite – had popped his trunk open to basically thumb his nose for getting pushed out. The young spirit then apparently moved on, and we forgot about him.

The next autumn, my daughter once again found some items in her room misplaced. She presented the findings to my wife to show her concern. My wife, fully aware of the young spirit, wrote it off to my daughter's absentmindedness and tried her best to ignore it. The next day my wife, just before entering the shower, closed the curtains in our bedroom. When she came out of the bathroom from showering and entered the bedroom again, the curtains were wide open. She second-guessed herself as to whether or not she'd actually closed them and forgot about it. The next evening she went to the downstairs bedroom, which was my mother-in-law's room. She was returning from a trip from Portugal, and my wife wanted to get her room back in order. As she cleaned the room, she came across a large metal ball that my son had. It came apart in two pieces, and he was storing toy cars in it at the time. My wife found a small green car on the floor and put it back inside the metal ball. She screwed it tight again and placed it back on the floor. When she turned around, she found the toy car on the carpet right beside the metal ball. Her logical mind told her that it was just another green car (as my son had several), and she figured that she had just missed it. Yet she never picked it up to see if it was the same car or to see if the one inside the metal ball had mysteriously "teleported" itself back to the carpet. She continued to tidy and found another green toy car on top of some sheets and blankets that she had just folded and put aside. That was enough for her.

I was at the movies with a friend when my phone went off. It was a text from my wife, explaining that things were moving around on her. She was scared, a little pissed, and wanted John and me to do something about it right then and there. I tried to watch the movie as much as I could (and not annoy the people around me) and texted John. He had crashed early, so he wasn't seeing his messages. After the show, I returned home, and my wife explained to me in more detail what had happened. I knew that it must have been this young spirit returning but wanted to confirm it with John.

The next day I sent him a photo of my daughter's room, and he quickly received a mental image of the kid in my daughter's room with his back to John. We quickly decided that it was time for him to go. That evening John connected to him and told me via text that the kid was walking around upstairs, going from room to room. I was in my basement in my recliner, waiting for the go-ahead. I closed my eyes and found the kid in the upstairs hallway that connected all the bedrooms and the main bath. As soon as I saw him, he headed into the bathroom. I followed him in (astrally) and cornered him between the toilet and the shower against the far wall. I grabbed him by the lapels of his jacket and projected the two of us out the door and into the street. I told him that he was no longer welcome in my home or any of the other homes in the immediate vicinity. He wouldn't make eye contact with me at all. I projected him towards the arboretum at the end of my street with one final warning never to return. I messaged John right after and asked him what he saw. John told me that he had seen the kid in the hallway outside a bedroom but he, "Just vanished." I told him what I had done, and he figured my "grabbing" him and dragging him away was why he lost quick contact with him.

A week later I was talking with a local psychic, DG. I told him all about the spirit and what had happened with my daughter and my wife. DG grew up in the area and had special gifts since he was very young. He would have been that kid who had imaginary friends and saw spirits from a very young age. He accepted his abilities and took it upon himself to become acquainted with the town's spirit population. He told me right away that the young spirit that John and I had dealt with was a fourteen-year-old who had committed suicide on the old train tracks behind a grocery store. These tracks were long gone and were now used for hiking and biking trails. The funny thing was that they were less than two hundred yards from my home. It made sense that he would be in the area and follow teenage girls around. DG said that this spirit's name was Jack, and he'd died during the Great Depression. That also would explain his clothing, as it looked dated, and because he was a suicide, he would most likely be afraid to move on for fear of eternal damnation. I wished now that I had spoken to him in a more reasonable fashion and not as a pissed-off husband and father. I would have tried to convince him to move on and not to be afraid of the next level of his existence. DG told me that if Jack ever came back and became a nuisance again, I was to call him, and he would take care of him. So far, so good...

29

KINCARDINE

K incardine is a beautiful town founded by Scottish immigrants on the shores of Lake Huron. It has miles of gorgeous beaches and is packed in the summer with vacationers. It also has a notoriety for being one of the most haunted towns in Ontario, and anyone with any sense of the paranormal can pick up on it as they drive around. Century homes in the Victorian style line the streets, and many of them give off an Addams family vibe as you pass them. It would be impossible NOT to find spirits in any of these homes.

A family in town were referred to John and me by a practicing shaman in the area. The shaman told us that this family were suddenly having issues with a malicious spirit in their home, and they were looking for help. The daughter, in her early twenties, whom I will call "Betty", was in the laundry room in the basement of the home. As she was folding clothes, an older lady spirit, who appeared to be in her late sixties, wearing a black dress, appeared before her. The spirit was burned all down the right side of her face, neck and shoulder. Betty attempted to flee the basement, but the spirit attacked her and clung to her as she tried to flee. The spirit then told Betty that she "wanted her to feel her pain". Betty shook her off and got out of the room and up the stairs as quickly as she could. The son in the home, also in his early twenties, was also visited by the same spirit. "Mark" told John and me that he would sense the burnt female spirit standing in the doorway of his bedroom every night as he tried to sleep. He would get negative implanted thoughts from her, and it had started to take its toll on him. He said that he could feel her anger as it permeated throughout his room as he tried to rest.

When John called me about the home and the malicious spirit, he told me about Betty seeing the burns on the right side of her face and body. As John gave me a description of the spirit and her "wounds", I got a warm and tingly sensation on the right side of my face, down my neck and all along my right arm and shoulder. This was before I knew where the actual burns had been. I then got a clear image of this lady, but she came to me wearing a very deep red dress not a black one as Betty had described. I then picked up on a mental image of their actual home. In my mind I could see a caramel-colored Victorian-style home on a corner lot of intersecting streets. An image of two lean tall men came to me as well. One had thick black glasses, brown hair and was wearing suspenders. The second man was standing behind him, but I couldn't get a clear image of him. I told John about the spirits that I picked up on, but for once he said that nothing like that came to him. This made me wonder whether I was actually seeing something with my gifts or just making it up in my imagination. I usually looked to John and his abilities for confirmation, but for once I couldn't.

A couple of days after John had called me about the home, I was up at his place, which is in the same area and not more than fifteen minutes from Kincardine. We were recording a podcast in his home, as Danny was unavailable that week, and the theater was off-limits. As we wrapped up our podcast, John's phone rang, and he saw that it was the mother, "Carla", who was calling. She gave us some information on the house and was eager for us to come up and see if we could help her and her family. We explained to her that we were both in the area and that now would be the perfect time for us to come up. She confirmed with her family that they were fine with it, and we set off right away.

As we pulled up to the house, I could see right away that it was just as I had seen in my mind. It was a beautiful home with gardens right out of a magazine. Caramel in color, as it had been in my vision, with a driveway at the back of the property. We could tell that there was a lot of pride and attention put into the place. Carla definitely had a green thumb and looked as if she spent a lot of time in the yard. As John and I walked up to the side entrance, we both became immediately short of breath and had tightening in our chests. Something was not happy with our arrival.

Carla greeted us at the door along with her husband, "Ben", and a monster of a dog. Carla gave us more details into what was going on in the house. We learned that they had just started to conduct some minor renovations in the home, and it was thought that that was what had stirred up the old lady spirit. As we stood in the kitchen and talked, I could feel myself being psychically attacked by something. I felt like I was standing on the deck of a swaying boat, my chest was tight, and I had tons of odd sensations going on throughout my entire body. John was being left completely alone at this time, and I was the only one being affected. Moments later, Betty and Mark joined us in the kitchen.

We discovered that the two "kids" both had abilities to see and/or sense spirits. Betty was especially sensitive and could see them all the time. She also seemed distant and slightly sad in her demeanor. She didn't make much eye contact with either one of us. I wasn't sure if that was just her natural demeanor, so I did my best to make light of the situation and tried to alleviate their fears. I worried that the attack on her might have affected her more than she had let on. Mark also came across a little distant and looked uncomfortable with our being there. We explained to them that we were there to help and would do everything we could for them.

The family took us on a tour of the gorgeous home and eventually led us upstairs to where the bedrooms were. As soon as I reached the top of the stairs, I looked down the hallway and could see a tiny woman sitting in a small rocking chair. She disappeared instantly, and I didn't mention it to anyone. I could sense that there were several spirits in the home and didn't want to say anything to upset anyone any further than they already were. As we all chatted in the hallway outside the bedrooms, I looked to my right slightly over my shoulder to a small landing at the end of the hallway. There I saw a young blonde girl in a white dress looking at me. Without thinking, I told everyone what I had just witnessed.

"Oh, that's Lilly," Betty said. "There are two child spirits here. Robby and Lilly. They died as adults but decided to come back as children. They're harmless and like to play on the stairs!"

I guessed right there that Betty was as sensitive (or more) than me, and it seemed that I didn't have to downplay what I saw in the home. Betty then asked me if I had seen the tiny lady in the rocking chair. I told her I had, and it was a nice confirmation for me that someone else was seeing the exact same things. John still wasn't being affected or sensing much of anything.

Mark stood at the opposite end of the short hallway with his back to his bedroom and bathroom. Behind him I could see the swoosh of a black dress and knew that the malicious old spirit had arrived to check us out. Moments later, I got a sharp poke in the back of my head, and I told everyone in attendance what I had just felt. Mark said that he had experienced that before and pointed to the exact spot on his head where he had felt it. It was the same location as mine. Something – possibly the old woman – was attempting to make its presence known.

We all descended the main stairs that led towards the front door, and I was last in line. As I walked down, I looked up and towards the small landing where I had seen the spirit of Lilly. There, on his knees and peering between the rungs, was obviously the little boy spirit Robby. He looked down at me with big brown eyes with a look of indifference on his face. His face wasn't lit up and didn't show any childlike innocence like I would have expected. When I joined everyone else again, I asked Betty if Robby had thick brown hair and big brown eyes, and she said that he did. Another positive confirmation. John and I continued our preliminary investigation and kept asking questions about the spirits in the home and the new activity. I could see other small childlike spirits running around the room and then saw one of the men in my "vision" standing in the doorway to a small office. There were literally a dozen spirits or more that I could sense. John said that he felt that the number was higher and there were close to eighteen in the home.

John then dropped a "bomb" on everyone. John had sensed the presence of something very tall, very dark, and very malicious in the basement of the home. It was different than the old woman, and he believed that it had followed Mark home from another location. Mark fessed up and said that he and friends had once sneaked into an old abandoned mental health facility in London, Ontario. Places like this are literal breeding grounds for dark entities, as they feed off the mental anguish and negative emotions of the patients. Being abandoned, it would have made for a perfect "home" for such demons to occupy. Mark also said that one of the girls in the group had received a huge scratch on her back from something unseen.

Betty then told us that she had witnessed a "black ooze" coming from the basement one evening, and it was coming out from under the door. John and I looked at each other, and we could both sense that we were excited about this one. The last stop of our house tour was the basement, where Betty had said that she was attacked by the old lady. I don't remember if she joined us down there at the time but wouldn't have blamed her if she had remained upstairs. John kept looking at one corner of the room we were in but stayed quiet for now.

John and I gave the family the best advice that we could in regard to protecting themselves for the time being. I explained to them that "Acknowledgment is Empow- erment", and to try their best to ignore anything that seemed to be paranormal. I also told Betty that one of the things I used to provide protection in my home and other places was to imagine a super shiny "disco ball" that starts off the size of a marble and continues to grow outward. As it gets bigger and bigger, its reflective surface pushes out any dark negative energy. It should eventually get so big that it consumes the entire home and property. John and I told them that we would do them that night remotely as well. We said our goodbyes and left the property. Once we left the house, I felt normal again and didn't have any chest pressure, head pain, or other odd aches. Whatever it was that was affecting me seemed to back off for now. Once John and I got back in the car, he told me that while we were talking to the family in the dining area, he kept getting a voice in his head that kept telling him to, *"Fuck off,"* and, *"Get the fuck out of the house."* He also told me that he had received a strong sense of dread from the basement.

The next evening it was time for John and me to perform our remote clearing. I texted him and told him to let me know where in the house the old lady was. Moments later he messaged me and said that she was on the first landing at the front stairway. I zeroed in on her and found her right where John had said she was. I set down beside her and wrapped my arms around her from the side. I told her over and over that she was to move on and that her husband would be waiting for her. I looked down at the bottom of the stairs and could see a nice-looking man in a tan suit looking up at us. I turned my attention back to her. I told her that it wasn't her place to be anymore and that she wasn't allowed to pass judgment on anyone in the family. To my left and just above the front doorway, I saw a cone-shaped tunnel appear. It tilted upwards toward the sky, and at its end I could see crackles of blue light emanating from it. Suddenly my arms felt lighter, and I could see two balls of white energy head up and through the tunnel. They disappeared at the far end, and I assumed that it was the old lady and her husband. Just then a third ball of energy entered the tunnel and began to move very slowly towards the crackling blue energy. It seemed to hesitate, backed up a bit, but then shot forward and vanished. The tunnel faded away, and I was back in my family room in my recliner again.

I messaged John and told him what had happened. He told me that the old lady vanished, and he assumed that I had done my "thing" and she was gone. What came next was very unexpected...

As John remote viewed the home, he was suddenly "pulled" into the basement. Something that neither one of us was expecting. He messaged me as it happened...

John – Look at the thing in the basement! Me – You there now?

John – Room beside furnace room. It's showing me the horns – whole bit

Me – I can't see shit...I'm not good with those guys. He still down there?

John – Fucking banging the walls of my house. Two guides just kicked me out

Me – Your own guides?

John – Yep. Said get out of here and they approached it. I just passed your uncle on the stairs. He pushed me up. I'm clearly out of my league here

Me – What about the old lady?

John – She is gone but I think she will come back. Might have to sick guides on her too. Gerry (one of John's guides) yelled at me to get out and said "What the fuck were you thinking?" Your uncle then shoved me up the stairs cause I wasn't moving fast enough

Me – Which uncle was it? I asked both to help John – I have no idea. He was mad as fuck. Stocky guy

This conversation came a few days later after going to the home in Kincardine...

John – So, this house in Kincardine, I think I'm going to let you be the lead on this. I've brought something real ugly here. Did you look in last night?

Me – Nope

John – I'm bowing out then

Me – Something really bad showed up at your place then?

John – Yep, two nights ago I was frozen in bed and couldn't even open my eyes. While I listened to something with hooves walk in and out of my bedroom. When I could finally open my eyes, my guides were carrying this thing out of the room and Burrel told me stop. She actually yelled it. She said, "Demon, smarten up!" I called the homeowner and told her I'm out.

Me – WOW

John – So this one is all yours or we can pass it on Me – We might have to call in the big guns

John – You decide what you want to do. If you don't want it then let's ask Michelle D if she can help or recommend someone

For the first time since the Big John spirit, John was rattled. I hadn't expected this but could tell obviously from his messages that this was something to be very aware of. For a moment I was nervous that John would want out of anything to do with the paranormal now – even the podcast. We both had these gifts for a reason and had helped many people with earthbound spirits and low-level poltergeists. This was something completely different. We both knew that one day we would run into something that we couldn't handle on our own, and it had come sooner than expected. I also had a guilty sigh of relief that this thing hadn't shown itself in my home. John had also openly expressed to Danny and me that he was trying to turn himself off to the supernatural and wanted a rest. There were weeks when we were both trying to clear several homes at once, and with him being the main lead, it was taking its toll. We were biting off more than we could chew and going full steam ahead. I told him, though, that this was a learning curve for us. We tended to bull our way into the spirits' domain and never considered the effects that it might have on us.

John then told me the details of what had happened at his home when the demon appeared. John explained that he could hear something quickly darting around his bed. It had hard feet and was tap-tap-tapping as it moved. When John tried to sit up and look to see what it was, he discovered that he couldn't move. He was experiencing sleep paralysis for the first time and was terrified. Something then pressed down on his chest, causing him to sink into the mattress a couple of inches. What happened next was awful. Something unseen reached into John's chest and stomach area, and it felt to him that his guts were being ripped out. He still couldn't move and felt panic rush through him. Suddenly the pressing feeling gave way, and he could move again. John looked to his left and could clearly see two of his guides literally dragging what looked like a goat with manlike arms and six-inch-long ram-style horns out his door. The beast looked back at him and only glared. He sat and watched the three of them disappear down the hall and through the wall.

John then told me that he had tried to make a deal with the demon. He said that he would stay away from the Kincardine home if it stayed out of his own home. Its reply was that if John didn't stay away, then it would do to his daughter what it had done to him. That was something that John couldn't bear to happen, and he openly agreed again to stay away. John was standing in his bedroom when this exchange occurred. On the far wall, there was a plaster footprint from his daughter that she had made in kindergarten. It was something that he cherished. As John looked, it started to swing on its hook from side to side. John's guide Burrel then came to him with a message for him to grab it before the demon smashed it. John quickly saved it from falling and placed it safely in a drawer.

The next evening we met at our usual watering hole before recording episode 15 of the podcast. I watched as John walked in holding his stomach, and he was slightly hunched forward like an old man. The pain from the thing tearing at his guts was like being tackled by a 250-pound lineman or being in a car accident, he said.

We recorded the podcast that night, and as I recall, we talked a little bit about the incident. Danny and I could tell that John wasn't himself that evening, and we both silently hoped that he would be okay.

John continued to be visited by this so-called demon for the rest of the week. It would drain his energy, scratch the walls, make knocking sounds, and move swiftly throughout his home. John messaged me and told me what was going on. Apparently the "deal" that he had made with this thing wasn't holding up, and it was doing as it pleased. *Never make a deal with the devil.*

I messaged John back and said that we had to find a way to

kick this thing's ass. I hoped that some of my bravado would transfer over to him and send a message to this dark entity that we weren't the kind of people who would bend over and take it dry. We were going to fight it and find a way to make it disappear once and for all. John also told me that he had opened up one of his kitchen cupboards one night to get something, and a small black cloud had shot out from the cupboard and flew over his head. He instantly knew it was this dark entity. John ramped up his own protection rituals and was doing them about three times a day. He was also smudging his home on a regular basis and was feeling better about himself and the energy in his home. Right after that, my wife and I kept getting drained at our home. We were both working from home at this time, and we were sleeping until one in the afternoon or later. We would both wake up, have something to eat, and felt like we could both go right back to sleep again. It was awful. We blamed each other for being lazy and being bad influences on each other, but I knew it was something else.

One of the nights I had a very weird dream where I was in my kitchen back in my old Caledon home. There was a large black slimy spider that was in one of the kitchen cupboards. I watched as it scampered away from me when I opened the door. It crawled over soup cans and jars of peanut butter as it tried to get to the back of the cupboard. Suddenly in my hand was a very shiny silver pair of tongs. I was able to reach in and grab the spider, go to the back door, and pitch it in to the backyard. The dream ended abruptly right after that. I took this as a sign that this thing that had been harassing John was now in my home, and I was to rid myself of it as quickly as I could. The same night, my daughter had a bad dream and was woken by her Xbox turning on all by itself. Her heater on her wall had been turned on as well. This was something I needed to deal with as soon as I could.

The next time that we recorded our podcast, John was feeling much better. His color had come back, and he was raring to go. He was ready to start viewing homes again and would have no problem with moving earthbound spirits. He told Danny and me that he had made a huge mistake at the Kincardine home. He told us again that when he and I were there and talking to the family in the kitchen, he kept getting a dark voice in his head, saying to "Get the fuck out of this house" and "Fuck off!" He ignored it and shouldn't have. It was a lesson learned the hard way, and he wouldn't make the same mistake again. John kept at it with his protection and smudged his home several times over the next week.

One night while sitting at home, and not much longer after John had his bad experience with this "demon", he messaged me. John told me that his daughter and her roommate were at their apartment in Toronto, and something frightening had happened to the two of them. The two girls had made coffee in a French press and had left the glass device on the counter. Two hours later, the press exploded as if something had hit it with a sharp object. The press wasn't heated or near anything that would make it shatter like that. It just broke on its own. Then the roommate, while studying, had a large lit candle on a stand. It suddenly flew into the air and came smashing down on the table in front of her, nearly spraying her with hot wax. The shower curtain, which was firmly bolted down, came free of its moorings and fell to the floor. Both girls were understandably frightened and had called John for help. He knew that this was the work of the Kincardine demon and was upset that it had targeted his daughter. John asked me to remote view their apartment, and I did so without question. I could instantly see the roommate, wearing a long-sleeved white shirt, sitting at a table, looking at a textbook. She was very thin and had long straight brown hair. I messaged John, described her, and asked if he could confirm that she was wearing a long-sleeved white shirt. John messaged his daughter and confirmed to me that she was wearing what I described. I positioned myself in the center of the room and filled the room with bright white light, trying to get it into every corner of the apartment. I also "disco balled" the place and had a good feeling afterwards that I had done something positive. John checked in with his daughter for the next week, and nothing ever happened again in the apartment.

30

THE GOVERNOR'S RESIDENCE

A fter conducting the investigation at the Wellington Museum, I was asked by a lady by the name of Janice to attend the Wellington City Council chambers and make a short presentation before all the mayors, councilors, and wardens that preside over our local communities. The presentation was to be a short talk presented by myself about the spirits of the building and what evidence we may have found. At the end of the presentation, I was to play our best EVP from the night.

The EVP that I chose was the demonic hiss/growl that we had captured in the old male infirmary. It was the area that we had chosen to set up our equipment and plan our evening. After speaking to the council chambers about the spirits of the museum, I cued the laptop, h it play, and blasted the growl through a set of speakers. It was a hit and certainly made everyone sit up and take notice. The warden was grinning from ear to ear but some of the other mayors looked a little pale from what they'd heard. Afterwards, a councilor approached me and told me that he was looking right at the mayor of my town when I played the growl. He told me that the mayor's eyes almost popped out of his head when he heard it. It made me grin hearing that.

Following the presentation, I was approached by a couple of ladies who worked in the building and was told that they were interested in having SHIP come in to conduct an investigation in the former Wellington County Courthouse now known as the Governor's Residence. The Governor's Residence is a separate building located behind the main chambers building and has a small quaint garden and courtyard between them. The original building was built in the mid 1800s and went through numerous changes and renovations for decades after. It used to have a small county jail in the basement, and now that same area serves as the treasury department for the county.

The Residence is a building that was noted to have a lot of paranormal activity. It was also a place where they had a hard time keeping cleaning staff, and people would report strong feelings of being uncomfortable in certain areas. I was even told that staff had reported that they had seen things move on their own, and there have been reports where people have seen ghostly figures peering out of the windows late at night. The courtyard was the spot of the local gallows and had several hangings back in the day when Canada still had the death penalty. Though records and "official" reports vary on the number of men who were executed in the city, I settled on the number six from my own findings.

Almost one year later, I contacted the staff who had initially inquired about an investigation and was once again greeted warmly. I had never come across such an eager group of people who were willing to have their space "invaded" by a group of ghost hunters before

– especially a government building. I was taken on a quick tour of the areas that we would have access to and met some more employees. The evening we were to come in was an election night for our surrounding municipalities. Our mayors and councilors would be elected and/or re-elected, so staff would be in the main building across from us, minding the data coming in from the polling stations. A young lady by the name of Christina was going to be our chaperone for the evening and even had a genuine interest in what we were doing and a belief in some aspects of the paranormal.

The team set up their base of operations on the top floor of the two-story building. The area was comfortable, with nice offices, a meeting area, a kitchenette, and a stairwell that went up to a rustic-looking attic. Tony and I set up a night-vision camera in the attic against the far wall with it facing most of the room and the entrance. It was only one of two cameras we had set up due to the layout of the building. Once we were set up, I asked Michelle and Corrine to begin their part of the investigation in the stairwell. One of the ladies who worked on the bottom floor had a friend who was psychic. Her friend came to visit her one day at work and came into contact with the spirit of a young woman who sat in the stairwell and cried all the time. We believed that this poor distraught female spirit was mourning the death of one of the men who were hanged on the property, and for some reason she couldn't move on. I hoped that the two female investigators might be able to communicate with her.

Tony and I began our evening in the attic and began to ask the possible spirits in the room questions with our recorders running. Within moments, I sensed two spirits come up the short stairs into the attic. As Tony stood in the middle of the room, we could hear something walking in circles around him. It literally sounded like footsteps on the hardwood floorboards going around and around. Like someone pacing. Tony, as usual, kept his calm and continued to ask questions. We didn't get any good audio from the attic, but our video evidence was another story.

Days later when Tony was going through the hours of video footage, he contacted all of us on Facebook messenger and told us we needed to see what he found. From the video footage from the attic, at the far corner of the room to the left of a supporting beam, a dinner-plate-sized shimmering anomaly, which looked like a man's face, appeared in thin air. The anomaly hovered in the air about six feet off the ground, moved behind the beam, and then came back and reappeared. It was an amazing piece of footage and something that the team had never captured before. This was exciting, as 99% of the time our videos never capture a thing. We often get orbs but never something as vivid as this.

The footsteps finally stopped in the attic, so Tony went to another area of the building while I went down to the main floor. The main floor had a nice reception and lobby area and a few small offices. I came down the elevator and entered the main area. As soon as I walked out, there was an office to my right. I began to head for the office, but something made me stop and turn towards the lobby. Entering that office just didn't seem right at that moment. I sat on one of the chairs and asked the spirits in the area to communicate through my digital recorder. Danny came out of the stairwell a short time later and couldn't see me sitting in the dark. I decided to let out a loud hiss to make him jump. He reacted just the way I wanted him to, and we had a quick chuckle over it. I watched him enter the office that I wasn't comfortable going to earlier. Moments later I heard him say that the energy in the room was heavy. I walked over to the office and entered the room. Suddenly the temperature in the room dropped by at least twenty points. It went from nice and warm to freezing within seconds. We were both shocked at the temperature change, as it was the first time we had ever experienced anything like that. We had always heard

about the temperature changes when dealing with the paranormal but had never faced it before. A minute later the room
became warm again, and we walked out of the office. As soon as
we crossed the threshold of the door, we could both smell feces.
Danny and I looked at each other and both agreed that there
was something nasty there with us. We had previously asked
John to remote view the building, and he'd told us that there
was "something dark" in the building. The nasty odor faded
away, and we retreated to the top floor to join the team.

The entire team gathered at a large meeting table on the top
floor. Our chaperone, Christina, was in her office just feet away
from us with her door closed. Tony turned on the spirit box, and
we asked the spirits to use their energy and speak to us through
it. As we took turns asking questions, we heard a man's disembodied voice, quite loud, come from the corner of the room that
was right outside Christina's office door. We all looked at each
other and collectively said, "What the hell was that?!" I walked
over to Christina's door, quickly knocked, and let myself in. She
sat there wide eyed, looking at me, and said, "I heard that!" I
confirmed that she hadn't been talking on the phone or
watching anything on her computer or phone that would have
been the source of the man's voice. She confirmed that she'd
been sitting at her desk quietly. Every member of the team had
their digital recorders going, and every one of us had captured
the man's disembodied voice. We played our recorders back and
could hear, loud and clear, a man say, *"Stop, stop. Whatever you're
doing, stop that!"* It was, to this date, our clearest EVP we had ever
captured. Our short investigation in the small building had
provided us with our best video evidence and our best audio
evidence.

31

SASQUATCH

Y eti, Yowie, Skunk Ape, Almas, the Grassman... There are many different names for the legendary Sasquatch from all over the world. In North America it is commonly referred to as Bigfoot. The elusive and legendary creature has a history in North America that dates back hundreds of years. North American Indians have been recording encounters with "Big Brother" on cave walls and passed on its legend from elder to elder. Even the infamous Viking Leif Ericson reported landing in the New World in AD 986 and coming face-to-face with "huge hairy men with black eyes".

As a huge fan of all things cryptid, it made sense that I would explore beyond my interest in ghosts and aliens and move on to the topic of Sasquatch. Looking for topics of interest for our podcast, I learned that John had a big interest in the legend of the hairy man as well, and we both sought to find some "experts" on the Bigfoot topic whom we could interview.

John was able to contact a couple from North Bay, Ontario, who had been investigating the creature for twenty years. Peter and Christine had both found each other late in life after losing their respective spouses to illnesses. They soon learned that they both had an affinity for the large hairy beast, and it may have actually drawn them to each other in an odd way.

Christine was a sensitive and had unfortunately suppressed her abilities for a long time. She had an encounter with a Bigfoot when she was a young girl in the town of South Porcupine, Ontario. She had gone berry picking on her own not far from her home and came face-to-face with what she now believes to have been a juvenile Sasquatch. As she had reached for some berries, a large brown-colored beast peeked up over the bush and locked eyes with her. They both froze for a few seconds, staring at each other, before Christine took off for home. That moment had a profound impact on her life and was the catalyst for her interest in the cryptid creature.

After having them both on our podcast, I arranged to go to North Bay and meet the two of them and go on my very first Bigfoot excursion. I met them at their home in the city and was greeted with trust and hospitality. I listened to their stories of going looking for the beast and looked at photos and plaster foot casts that they had collected.

As we spoke at their dining room table, I could get the sense that there was a spirit in the room with us. Peter and Christine had both recently lost their spouses, so I assumed that it was either Christine's husband or Peter's wife. As we spoke across the table from one another, Christine and I saw a massive shadow man run full tilt across the living room. Peter had his back to the room and didn't see anything. Christine and I both looked at each other and said, "What the hell was that!?" Peter just smirked and said something about "us gifted people". I could see that the shadow man had upset Christine a bit, as she looked anxious, but I changed the subject and kept the conversation going about Bigfoot.

While we continued to talk at the dining room table, I noticed the hair at the top of Christine's head rise as if someone had run their fingers through her hair. She looked at me and said she felt something touch the top of her head. I told her that I saw her hair move, and then a moment later I felt a presence touch the top of my head as well. We both shrugged it off and quickly dismissed it.

A couple of days before I had headed north, Tony had asked John and me to remote view Bigfoot. It was something that I had never considered and was glad that he had brought it up. John messaged me and told me that he had already done it, and he would wait to see me in person before sharing with me what he had seen. I settled into my recliner, closed my eyes, and focused. Within seconds I found myself "floating" over a wooded area that had a rock face and what appeared to be some water nearby. Peter and Christine hadn't told me anything about the area that we would be investigating yet, so I had nothing to go by. The thing that struck me about the area that I was viewing was that it was all in full color. That had never happened to me, as usually everything was in a type of black-and-white visage. This suddenly changed, as I was now standing on the forest floor, and everything was black and cobalt blue. The "air" was black, but everything else – the trees, bushes and ground – was a cobalt blue. As I settled, an actual blueish doorway opened up in front of me. Standing in the door was a very large form of what appeared to be a Bigfoot. This thing was looking right at me and knew I was there. It didn't look very happy about my presence. It continued to look at me for a few more moments and then stepped out of the "door" and walked away to my left. Next a smaller-looking creature came out, followed by what appeared to be a female Sasquatch. The young one walked right up to me and literally put its face right in mine. It tilted its head back and

forth almost like in a state of curiosity. If this had been a physical meeting, I would have smelled its breath for sure. The
female came up behind the adolescent, pulled it away (with a
seriously pissed-off look), and walked off in the same direction
that the first one had. To my amazement, three more beasts
came out of the doorway. They were bigger than the first one,
and all appeared to be male. The males all had cone-shaped
heads, while the female and youth had flat-topped heads. They
were certainly aware of my presence and scowled at me while
they passed and walked off in the same direction as all the
others. I then snapped my eyes open and sat in stunned silence
in my family room as I tried to soak in what had just happened.

I had to go see John at his home for some podcast-related
work and told him what I had witnessed. John then told me that
when he had remote viewed the forest around North Bay, that
he had settled on the forest floor, and everything was black and
white, not black and blue like I had seen. John told me that he
had appeared behind a very large Bigfoot, and its back was
turned to him. John also said that as soon as he "appeared", the
beast sensed that he was there and stopped walking. John said it
stopped in its tracks, turned its head slightly toward him, and
then raised a huge hairy arm to dismiss him. John said that
whatever this creature did, it had cast him off immediately, and
John found himself back in the reality of his living room. John
marveled at the way the Sasquatch had dismissed him almost in
a psychic way. We haven't tried to remote view the creature
since.

Peter and Christine told me that the area where we would be
going to wasn't far from the city, and we would be joined by a
father and son team of investigators. Jim was the father, and
Andrew was the son, a young man in his mid twenties. They
both knew the area that we were going to very well and had
interacted with and had even witnessed a Sasquatch two years

ago. We would be meeting with them at 0500 hours at our undisclosed location.

0430 came quickly, and I didn't get a bit of sleep. The couple had offered me the use of their couch in the basement instead of my getting a motel in the area. Peter came down to get me, and we headed out. It was early November, and there had been a fresh snowfall the past couple of days. It wasn't very cold out, but there were a few inches of snow on the ground. We met with Jim and Andrew at the location we were to investigate and set off down a trail leading into thick bush. The fresh snow and the foggy sky allowed the lights of the city to illuminate the area, and we didn't need flashlights.

Jim stopped about a hundred yards down the trail to show me where he had seen the Sasquatch a couple of years ago. He said it had appeared before him about twenty yards away and was at least nine feet tall. It had hesitated briefly, giving him a good look, before lumbering away. I had marveled at how close it had been at the time. Jim continued to explain to me how he and Adam would take a hard piece of wood and do some tree knocking. This is something that researchers often do in hopes of communicating with the creatures. They told me that they often got responses back, and I hoped that we would this morning. Andrew would walk along the trail, and every eighty yards or so, he would knock on a tree a couple of times. We all strained to listen for a response but didn't get anything back. For the purposes of the podcast, I carried a recorder with me and narrated as I went along and hoped to get something on audio.

As the five of us trundled along in the snow through the forest, there were spots where we could see small bright "orbs" of light moving through the trees. They certainly weren't insects due to the time of year and the weather. We watched one that was across a small swampy area move along the trees a couple of feet off the ground. Many people who have had Bigfoot encounters have admitted to seeing colored orbs moving through the forest at the same time. The theory is that the creatures can control their vibrational rate and "disappear" when they want to. When they do this, they project a small energy orb. We watched this orb vanish into the trees, and we continued along the trail.

I stopped Jim for a moment and, with my recorder going, asked him how many Sasquatches he believed were in this particular location. He had been coming in here for years and communicating with them and leaving gifts, so I figured he had a pretty good idea as to how many were in here. What he said next amazed me. Jim told me that he believed that there were four males, a female and an adolescent! That was exactly what I had encountered when I had remote viewed them in this same location. He continued to tell me that they always had two acting as sentinels to watch out for people coming into the area and would warn the others either through knocks or whistles. I grinned like an idiot in the dark, thinking about what I had seen and Jim pretty much confirming it. I didn't tell him about my viewing, as the topic was still something that I didn't reveal to too many people due to the fantastic nature of it all. We continued plodding through the snow.

I got ahead of the group and came to a spot where the trees thinned out and you could see more clearly through them. The forest floor sloped upwards slightly and went to a small rise, which was thick with evergreens. I stopped and stood looking at the evergreens, as something was drawing me to the spot. I just felt compelled to stare at the thickets of trees ahead of me up the gentle slope. Christine caught up to me, and we both watched as a small orb slid through the trees before disappearing. She then told me that she was being drawn to the area ahead of us and felt like we were being watched. I confirmed the same and kept my eyes straight ahead. Peter, Jim, and Andrew caught up to where Christine and I were standing. Jack told me that this was their "gifting" area. He would often leave jars of peanut butter, chocolate, carrots, nuts, and other goodies for the Bigfoot. I wondered aloud if that was why Christine and I had stopped at the exact location. We definitely felt like we were being watched.

Andrew gave out a few knocks with his stick, and we all waited for a response. Nothing. Andrew then gave out a couple of quiet whistles towards the evergreens. From the trees we received an exact response. Something mimicked Andrew's whistle right back to us. We all grinned and looked at each other. Andrew then tapped lightly on a tree beside him. A light tapping noise came from the same location exactly like Andrew had done. We were excited to get a response. This wasn't any kind of bird or even a human playing a trick on us. It was five in the morning in the middle of the bush in November. Moments later we could all see, about eight to nine feet up in the thick of the trees, what appeared to be three sets of eyes looking back at us. The eyes were black, and the lights of the city glinted off them. They remained for about thirty seconds and then slowly moved back farther into the trees and the darkness. We quietly speculated as to what we all had witnessed before something distracted us. Right behind our group were three deer silently standing not more than ten feet away from us. You could almost literally spit on them, they were so close. The deer just stood and looked at us and didn't make any effort to flee. I have been around deer as a hiker and a hunter and have never seen deer remain this calm and this close to people. Christine then said that she believed that the Sasquatch had been hunting the deer, and we were between them. The deer probably felt safe with us acting as a barrier. It was a logical statement, and we collectively agreed on it. We continued along the trail without any further excitement and made it back to our vehicles.

The five of us found a truck stop nearby for some very early morning breakfast. We all chatted about Bigfoot and other paranormal phenomena between bites. It had been an exciting morning and a fantastic first experience for me. I told the group that I would love to come back and investigate some more in the spring. Ghosts, aliens, and now Bigfoot. All I had to do now was to find the Loch Ness monster.

32

REMOTE VIEWING

I wasn't going to add this to the book, but after some consideration, I figured I should at least have some information and perspective on the matter. By official definition, remote viewing (RV) is the practice of seeking impressions about a distant or unseen target using extrasensory perception (ESP). It was something that governments, the USA specifically, invested a lot of money in to see if they could use people's remote viewing skills to spy on targets. The "Stargate" project was started in 1978 and ended (at least on paper) in 1995, as the CIA felt that it wasn't useful in intelligence gathering. I am speculating here, but I am more than certain that this is an ongoing practice to this day.

When John and I began to use our "gifts" to remote view people's homes and establishments, it was never something that I ever trained for, or ever considered that I could do. We actually only call it "remote viewing" because we couldn't come up with any other official term for it. The "actual" method of remote viewing consists of a random set of "co-ordinates" written on a piece of paper and then given to a test subject. That person then uses those numbers to locate and describe an actual location or event anywhere in the world. That person then typically sketches out what they viewed on paper. Certainly not the same as what we do.

What John and I basically do is look at a photo sent to us of a location, and then go there in our minds. We don't leave our bodies, as some people do with an out-of-body experience. There's no flying like Superman across the sky – although that would be very cool. We focus on the place we want to go, and BAM, we're there. Sometimes it's very easy and clear, and other times it's hard to focus and very muddled. We can also go "in and out" of the location and take the time to text each other back and forth about what is going on at the location. The fact that we see spirits when we RV is an added "bonus". I have never seen the living when I have done this. As far as I know, John has only seen an actual living person once – so far.

As cool and far out as remote viewing seems, there are some inherent dangers to it as well. John and I found this out the hard way. Since it was something that just happened for us and we never received any real guidance or training, we just jumped in headfirst. Our beautiful and very knowledgeable friend Michelle Desrochers gave us proper shit when she found out that we weren't getting rid of the trail that we left back to our own places (more on this in the next chapter). We were being successful in ridding homes of "nasties" but, unbeknownst to us, we were basically letting them follow us home. Thankfully, (sorry, John) the majority of them went to his place and not mine. I think that my spirit uncles were probably running inter-ference a lot for me and my family and zipping around the house knocking ghostly heads as they went. They're good at that sort of thing...

For now, John and I have shut down the remote viewing for a

while until we learn to properly defend ourselves and get rid of the trail we leave behind. We will, though, educate ourselves and go in with a proper game plan from now on. The learning curve continues.

33

SO YOU WANT TO BE A GHOST HUNTER…

A s I stated before, I am by no means an expert on the paranormal. I may be more experienced than your average person, but I still seek out answers to questions that I have and rely heavily on the experience of others. I can offer advice that I can pass on from friends or relay my own firsthand accounts and tell you what might have worked for me. Every little bit helps, right?

Often when I am out and about, I get into conversations about the topic of ghosts. It's become a part of my life, so it's only natural to speak about what interests you might have. I will sometimes be in someone's home, establishment, or some other location and pick up on a ghostly presence. Being the outgoing and forward person that I am, I will ask whoever owns the place or whoever works there about the ghosts in the building. More often than not, I get a wide-eyed look and a nervous awkward response. That's when I know that they have seen something there, and I have just opened the door for some fun, yet serious, conversation. The pub that we always meet at before we record our podcast has several spirits running around and something dark and nasty in the basement. The female servers always go down in pairs whenever they need to get supplies or tap a new keg. There is one young lady there who is nervous about the topic, yet interested, and I always greet her with, "What's with the ghosts in this place?"

She always laughs (nervously) and then gives me hell for always bringing the topic up. Even though she expresses some fear towards the subject, she has asked us to take her along on an investigation. I then joke that we are going to lock her in the basement of a location and come back for her in the morning. Random people and new acquaintances often ask me if they can attend one of our investigations. They have their own reasons for wanting to come along, whether it's curiosity, that adrenaline rush I spoke of, or a guarded secret interest. The problem is, hunting for spirits is not something that you should ever take for granted.

Inevitably, when you are searching out spirits, you will take something home with you that you don't want to. This may be a regular spirit, poltergeist, nonhuman entity, or something far worse. Whether you think you have any psychic abilities or sensitivity to spirits or not, your "antenna" will go up, and you will put out a virtual signal that you are opening yourself up to the spirit world. Fellow podcast host Danny always stated that he never saw anything or felt anything when he started investigating with SHIP. But after a while he began to see peripheral movement in locations, shadow people, and even had some strange occurrences at home, where lights turned off on their own and his sound system began to act oddly on its own. He also began to see orbs with his naked eye moving around the Harriston Theater when he was in there alone. He expressed excitement about his "opening up" to the spirits, but also expressed concern as well. Smart man. For many years, I shut myself down, lowered my antenna, and experienced virtually nothing at all. It wasn't until I became involved with SHIP that I opened up once again and became a magnet for the paranormal. This wasn't something that I was concerned about at all but came to realize that I should have educated myself a bit more before jumping in headfirst.

Tony, as well, has taken some not-so-nice things home with him and has suffered for it. We all have. Attachments can be an awful thing to have and often an even harder thing to get rid of. John once went to a shaman in his area to see what she might be able to clear from him. As he lay on her table, she began to conduct her clearing rituals. The shaman then told John that she "took a dagger" out of his side, a "clamp from around his neck", and saw an astral mouse come out of his throat – *something that she had never experienced before.* She said that the dagger and clamp were the work of the Big John spirit, but the source of the mouse was a mystery. While she finished up what she was doing, an object came flying off her shelf. This was also something that she had never experienced before when clearing someone. When it was all said and done, John said he felt like a million bucks when he got off her table. Unfortunately for John, this was a temporary feeling because as he continued to remote view people's homes and assist them with their own attachments, he was inviting more things into his own home at the same time. Michelle Desrochers warned both of us that we weren't taking the proper measures when remote viewing, and we were leaving a virtual "trail of bread crumbs" back to our own homes. The spirits and nasties that we were booting out were just following us back home, and this was something we needed to avoid. In our defense, we told Michelle that no one had ever warned us about what we were doing, and we had just dove right in. This was a learning curve for John and me, and we had to educate ourselves right quick. I know I already mentioned this in the last chapter but figured I needed to remind myself about what a nitwit I was.

Attachments often are negative in nature. Malicious spirits or dark entities look to people to feed off of for their own mysterious gains. The dark and ominous entities basically use us as food and thrive off our energy. People will often claim that they lack any kind of vitality in their haunted home and often wake up exhausted. They are being oppressed at every level. Investigators must be aware of their "psychic antennas" going up when they enter a supposedly haunted location. Your mind opens up in such a way that you become a magnet for spirits, and they are drawn to you like moths to a flame. Most will hold back and watch to see what your purpose is and see if they wish to communicate or not. They are – at least most of them – deceased people who still have free will. If they want to interact with you, they will. They aren't trained monkeys.

If you do decide to join a paranormal group and go look for spirits, then you must do everything that you can to protect yourself. There are several things that you can do to help keep yourself clear and choose what you feel works the best. It's not so much the "mystical" properties that some things have to ward off spirits, but the strong intent that is behind them. For religious people, a cross, St. Michael's medallion, or prayers might be the thing that works for them. They strongly believe in the power behind them, and this is where the intent comes into play. If you don't have a strong belief in religious articles, then they will not work for you. At the Clifford home, when Melissa and her husband were being tormented, she sprinkled holy water around the home after receiving a bottle of it from a relative. The spirit took the bottle from the top of the fridge and placed it on the lid of the garbage can. This was a strong indication that the water wasn't effective, and he was basically telling her off in his own way. Apparently, Melissa's belief and intent in the water wasn't strong enough.

Others believe in the use of crystals and gems such as black tourmaline, bloodstone, emerald, and labradorite. I have some small rocks of black tourmaline at home that I use at times. Crystals and gems need to be "recharged" quite often, and one way to do this is to leave them under the full moon for the night, or throw them in your freezer for a few hours. Any negative energy they may have collected will come right off and be useless.

Selenite lamps, I have been told, are very effective in helping to ward off psychic attacks from spirits. Selenite is a crystallized form of gypsum and is believed to help shield people and homes from negative outside influences. When John was harassed by the Hat-man demon, a very skilled clairvoyant told him to get a lamp for his room. The very night he plugged it in, John was awoken by a voice and told to look outside. When he did, he could see the Hatman standing outside on his back lawn, looking up at him. I don't believe he has been back since. The lamp did its job, and it continues to glow in John's room every night. You can also purchase small selenite "wands". These are just small cigar-shaped crystals that you can place on your window ledges and above your doorways to help keep negative energy out of your home. (See John's book for more on the Hatman.)

The psychic who told my mother about the malicious ghost in my boyhood home told her that if he ever felt that there was something negative in his home, or if he was in a hotel and couldn't sleep, that he would take salt, pour it into a glass of warm water, stir it with a spoon, and then sprinkle the liquid around the location. According to him, spirits hate salt water, and this was a good way of clearing them out of the area. I have also heard of people pouring salt in the corners of every room for a couple of days to absorb any negative energy. Just be sure to collect it and dispose of it outside your home.

Sage is another popular item to use to protect yourself and your home. The process, called "smudging", is where you light one end of the sage and, using your hand or a feather, walk in a clockwise pattern around your home and push the smoke away from you. Let the smoke get in to all the corners, nooks, crannies, and everything in between. As you go along from room to room, you use your positive intent and command any and all negative energy to leave your place. Start in the basement and don't forget to get into the crawl spaces, closets, and (if you can) the attic and garage. Make sure you open a couple of windows so the negative energy can escape. You can also sage yourself as well – especially right after an investigation.

John and I have our own protection rituals that we do, but we often forget to do them and get complacent about what we are doing. We have both learned the hard way that there are steps we must take to protect ourselves. There have been many times where I will remotely enter a location and put my "disco ball" out. This is where I envision a small reflective ball of bright white light in the center of the location that I am at. I then slowly expand that ball of light and make it bigger and bigger. Its reflective surface repels and pushes out any dark energy that may be there. As it grows and grows, the disco ball fills with the brightest white light that I can imagine. It spreads so large that it engulfs the entire home and forms a protective barrier around the place. I will know that it has worked because I will get a very satisfying feeling wash over me. It's hard to explain, but I will just know that it has done the job for the time being.

The human mind is more powerful than we give it credit for. Although this "disco ball" of light can only be seen by me in my mind's eye, its powerful intention emits a certain energy that can undeniably be felt.

One day I met with psychic pal DG at a local coffee shop, as he was a whiz at editing video and had the software and programs to do so. I have zero skills when it comes to things like that, so he was more than happy to help out. The video footage was something that I had filmed at the Harriston Crown Theater during a very short mini investigation that John, Tony, Danny and I had conducted. A production company wanted to see us in action and how we operated. I gave DG the SD card from my camera, and he inserted it into his laptop. For several minutes, DG fumed and fussed over the fact that his laptop wasn't cooperating and wouldn't recognize my SD card. He was getting increasingly frustrated and couldn't figure out what was wrong. For some reason the thought popped into my head that there was something from the spirit world that was making the laptop not work. I focused in my chair across from DG and projected a large ball of protective light around us, and a smaller one around the laptop. As soon as I did this, the laptop miraculously started to work. DG gave out a triumphant, "Yes!" and began to work his editing magic. Being a psychic medium himself, I then told DG what I had just done. He completely understood, gave a thumbs-up, and went to work. My intent was for the ball of protective light to work, and it did.

Grounding yourself is a very important thing to do before walking in to a possible haunted location. Grounding can help you protect yourself from unwanted attachments and connects you to Mother Earth. To ground yourself, visualize a bright ball of energy at the top of your head. Slowly move the ball down into your body. As it moves slowly down, imagine that it collects negative energy like a magnet. Move the ball of magnetic energy down, down, down as it expands into your shoulders, down your arms and down your torso. It collects the negative energy and continues slowly down into your lower body, pelvis, legs, calves and feet. Once it has reached your feet, envision roots growing from your feet and spread them down as far as you can into the earth. The negative energy will then be dispersed into the ground and neutralized. Once all the negative energy is gone, then slowly draw the ball of energy back up into your body, into your feet, up your legs, torso, and arms to your head until the white light completely fills your body. When you are finished and have done this correctly, you will definitely feel an improvement. Believe me, it works. Even if you aren't ghost hunting, this is something that you should make a habit of and do every day.

There have also been times where I have sensed a negative spirit nearby and have visually surrounded it in a purple ball of light. I imagine that the inside of the ball is reflective like a mirror or like the inside of a thermos. If it tries to propel any negativity towards me, then the reflective interior will just bounce it right back at it. The color purple is also associated with Michael the Archangel, and I have found that it is an easy color to conjure in my mind.

You also have to realize that not all spirits are bad or have evil intentions. They might move things just to get a rise out of you. Or it might be their way to get your attention, and they are seeking to communicate with you. If someone was a bit of a prankster in life, then they might certainly carry that over in death. I can guarantee you that if I die tomorrow and am able to come back as a mischievous spirit, then a lot of people are getting pinches on the butt. I also might spend some time floating around the Playboy Mansion as well. Just sayin'...

If you have something in your home that you want to deal with and rid yourself of, then you must remember that emotions are huge for spirits to feed off of. You need to keep yours in check when dealing with them or when living with them. Even an angry burst of bravado that you feel might be effective just fuels them as much as fear does. Remember – "Acknowledgment is Empowerment". I'm not asking you just to accept their presence in your home, but you must do everything in your power to ignore what may be going on around you until the time comes that you can do something to get rid of them. Some people just accept their spirits and the activity that comes with it. The family of the Dufferin County farmhouse have had numerous incidents that would make any other family head for the hills and slap that for sale sign on the end of the driveway. They are strong-willed professionals, take things in stride, and remain in their beautiful home.

Calling on a respected medium or shaman can clear your home as well. You must have the intention within yourself though that you truly want them to clear the negative energy out of your home. As Michelle Desrochers once told me, they can come back if they really want to. There is no perfect formula for ridding yourself of them. You can, however, make it seriously irritating and uncomfortable for them to the point that they give up and move on to another location.

So now that you've read all that and taken it in, you are going to be stubborn and still want to be a paranormal investigator... Good, there's more...

So, where do you begin? The best thing to do is to find an already established paranormal group in your area. Find them on Facebook, Kijiji, and Craigslist and send them a message. If by chance they need some members, then you have to realize that they might expect you to purchase some of your own equipment, and let me tell you, ghost hunting is an expensive hobby. One investigator I know spent over $20,000 in two years on equipment. You, though, might expect to spend a couple of hundred dollars off the hop. A digital recorder, K2 meter, flashlight, and camera are usually the basics. Then you will have to download an audio computer program to listen to all the EVPs you may have captured. You will spend hours upon hours sitting mindlessly in front of a computer, listening for the slightest audio anomaly. Your eyes will bug out of your head, your butt will ache, and your back will stiffen. Exciting stuff, I know.

As for the actual investigation, you will most likely find yourself sitting on the floor of a bedroom in some stranger's house, asking questions to no one in particular. The husband of the home will insist that he can't miss one minute of the hockey or baseball game and will listen to it with the sound blasting – effectively ruining most of your audio recordings. The wife will most likely want to follow you around and talk your ear off until you kindly and very politically tell her to shut her trap. The family dog will bark and scamper around the house, which will also add to your audio frustrations. It will most likely be a Saturday night, and after about an hour into the investigation, you will wish you were at the bar with your friends or had gone to a movie instead. If you are really lucky, the family will offer you a coffee or a snack. Two to six hours later, you will pack everything up, say your goodbyes, and try to stay awake behind the wheel as you head for home.

Weeks will go by, and you will make every attempt to coordinate with your teammates a good night to go over any evidence you may have found. Finally, you will get together (except for that one person) and sit and listen to everyone's EVPs that they captured. Then you will all hear something completely different than the others sitting at the dining room table with you, and the polite arguing begins. One of you hears the spirit say, "That's for me..." one of you will hear, "Outside is a tree..." and one of you will hear, "Hail Satan, the dark overlord!" (There's always that one person, trust me.) Then comes the video review, where you will bicker over the light anomalies drifting through the air. One light anomaly will shoot through the air, do an S turn, perform aerial acrobatics, and then zip up and through the ceiling. And that "one person" will say, "Oh, that's just dust..."

So there you have it. As honestly and sincerely as I could put it all together. All that excitement and experience in less than two years. I can only imagine where the next two years take me. Every word is true, and I am true to my word. Just remember one thing – spirits are everywhere. Just check over your shoulder...

ABOUT THE AUTHOR

Growing up in a haunted home, Dan is no stranger to the paranormal and what lies beyond the veil. Instructed by a psychic-medium to avoid all things supernatural until he was twenty-one years old, Dan's interest in the paranormal became all but forgotten until a chance meeting with a new neighbor. An introduction to a local paranormal investigative team sent him on his current path today.

Today, Dan is now part of SHIP (Strange Happenings Investigators of the Paranormal) a cohost of a popular podcast called The Phantom Faction, appeared on several paranormal television programs, radio shows and podcasts, and penned the nonfiction book, Strange Happenings: A Paranormal Investigators Story.

Made in the USA
Columbia, SC
05 March 2022

57233212R00145